R I C E

MARY GOODBODY

PHOTOGRAPHY BY

GENTL & HYERS

CollinsPublishersSanFrancisco
A Division of HarperCollins*Publishers*

First published in USA 1995 by Collins Publishers San Francisco
1160 Battery Street, San Francisco, CA 94111

PRODUCED BY SMALLWOOD & STEWART, INC., NEW YORK CITY

© 1995 Smallwood & Stewart, Inc.

RECIPE DEVELOPMENT: Rick Rodgers
ASSISTANT RECIPE DEVELOPMENT: Peter Goodbody
EDITOR: David Ricketts
FOOD STYLING: Frances Boswell
PROP STYLING: Edward Kemper Design
BOOK DESIGN: Susi Oberhelman
DESIGN ASSISTANT: Pat Tan

Library of Congress Cataloging-in-Publication Data

    Goodbody, Mary.
        Rice / Mary Goodbody.
            p.   cm. — (The gourmet pantry)
        Includes index.
        ISBN 0-00-225215-5
        1. Cookery (Rice)   I. Title.   II. Series.
    TX809.R5G63   1995
    641.6'318—dc20   95-5952

PRINTED IN ITALY

10 9 8 7 6 5 4 3 2 1

CONTENTS

INTRODUCTION

Rice is deliciously versatile. It can be baked into bread, made into pancakes, used for classic dishes such as risotto and pilaf, and tossed into soups. It figures in the culinary heritage of most of the world's cultures and many of its great cuisines.

The recipes in this book incorporate rice into daily meals, in a variety of delicious ways. Here you will find easy, approachable dishes that make good use of the wide array of rices on the supermarket shelves. There are recipes for long-grain white rice (the most commonly consumed rice in the United States) for brown rice, for medium-grain rice, for sticky rice, and for wild rice (even though this last is not truly a rice!). There are also recipes for the more exotic such as arborio, basmati, and jasmine rices.

When possible, use the right kind of rice for the dish; but if you cannot, try to make an educated substitute. For example, the Paella calls for medium-grain rice, preferably a Spanish-style rice to be authentic. But if you can only find Asian-style medium-grain rice, use that rather than long-grain converted rice. Usually the recipe has evolved because of the type of

rice locally available, not the other way around. (A friend from Cuba explained that the recipe on which we based Caribbean Black Beans & Rice for medium-grain rice because "it's what we had available at the market.")

There is no reason to rinse American-grown rice, unless the recipe specifies to do so. Imported rice, however, often benefits from rinsing, simply because packaging regulations are not always as stringent in other countries as they are here. You should rinse the rice under cool running water until the water runs clear, or soak it in a bowl with enough water to cover, stirring the rice and changing the water until it looks clear.

Store all rice in a cool, dry cupboard. Rice dries out with time, so it may take more or less time to cook than given in the recipes on pages 11 to 15. Once cooked, rice does not keep at room temperature for more than a few hours. It can be stored in the refrigerator, but should be reheated with a little liquid rather than consumed cold, as it tends to harden in the center during refrigeration. There are a few exceptions (see the rice salads), and fried rice must be made with chilled rice.

This book is written in the belief that we will all eat better and live more healthfully by cooking with all kinds of rice.

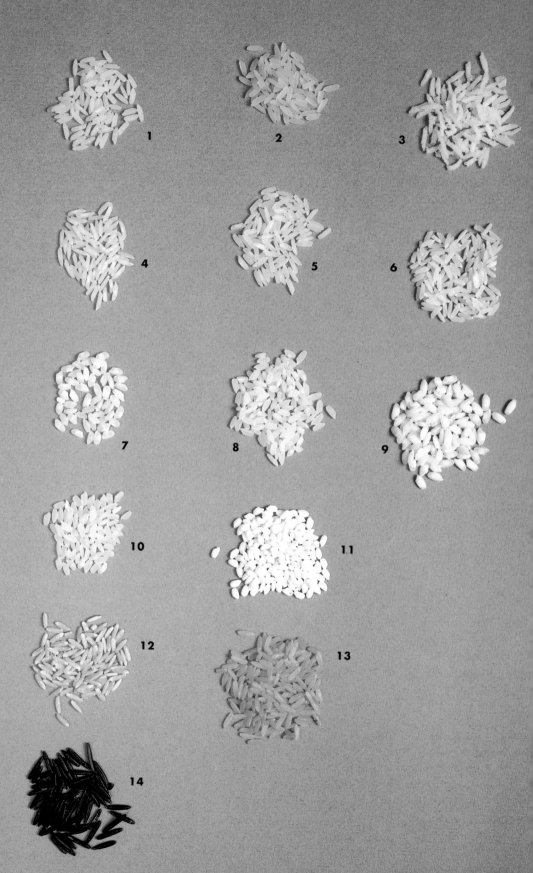

GLOSSARY

ARBORIO RICE (9)

Probably the most commonly available Italian medium-grain rice (often mistakenly described as short-grain), arborio is prized for making risotto and other dishes that require a firm-textured yet creamy rice.

AROMATIC RICE (4, 5, 6)

Appreciated for their nutty flavor and fragrant aroma, aromatic rices are long-grain and usually white with some brown types. Those commonly available are basmati, popcorn-style, and jasmine. Popcorn-style tastes distinctly of popcorn.

ASIAN-STYLE RICE (10)

These are medium- and short-grain rices, with a high percentage of the starch, *amylopectin*, which imparts a sticky and relatively soft consistency to cooked rice, a texture preferred throughout Asia. The Asian-style rices sold in Asian markets and many supermarkets in this country are all medium-grain. Some domestic rice growers, particularly on the West Coast, grow similar rices, giving them Asian names or otherwise indicating they are Asian in style.

BASMATI RICE (4, 12)

This long-grain rice, grown in India and Pakistan, is valued for its flavor and aroma. When cooked, the rice elongates instead of plumping, which results in long, narrow grains that are dry and separate. The latter two qualities are attributable to the 1 to 2 years that basmati is aged. Available as both white or brown rice, basmati should be cooked as long-grain white or brown rice. Basmati rice is grown in this country, but only in small amounts, although growers expect their outputs to increase in the coming years.

BROWN RICE (12, 13)

Brown rice requires longer cooking than white rice because only the inedible husk has been removed, leaving the outer shell (bran) intact, which acts as a barrier to heat and moisture. The bran layer colors the rice beige, and when cooked, the rice tastes nutty and is chewier than white. Brown rice is touted by many for its health benefits, especially its higher fiber and vitamin E content than white. Most commonly bought as a long-grain rice, it is also available as medium- and short-grain. Because of the high oil content in the bran layer, brown rice should be kept no more than 3 months, preferably in the refrigerator, to avoid it becoming rancid.

CONVERTED RICE (2)

See Parboiled Rice

INSTANT, QUICK, OR PRECOOKED RICE (3)

These terms refer to rice that has first been milled, then completely cooked and dried. The resulting rice requires just a short time in boiling water to rehydrate. Although convenient, it does not share the flavor or texture of other rice.

ITALIAN-STYLE MEDIUM-GRAIN RICE (9)

Italian-style rices are medium-grain white and contain a high level of *amylopectin*, a starch that makes them creamy when cooked. The grains, however, do retain a firm inner core. Italian-style rices, mostly grown in Northern Italy, include arborio, carnaroli, and vialone nano.

JASMINE RICE (5)

An aromatic long-grain white rice, jasmine rice was originally cultivated in Thailand, but is now successfully grown in this country. It is exceptionally fragrant and moist when cooked.

LONG-GRAIN RICE (1, 2, 4, 5, 6, 12, 13)

The term long-grain applies to any rice, white or brown, that is more than three times longer than it is wide. Common long-grain rices include American converted or parboiled, basmati, and jasmine.

MEDIUM-GRAIN RICE (7, 8, 9, 10)

White or brown and slightly shorter than long-grain rice, medium-grain rice is plumper looking. When cooked, it is soft and tender and is used in dishes where the rice is meant to absorb much of the flavor of the other ingredients, as in *arroz con pollo* and paella. Rice labeled "sushi rice" is medium-grain rice, often imported from Asia.

PARBOILED RICE (2)

This term applies to rice that has been soaked, steamed, and dried before milling, as a means of preserving nutrients that would otherwise be lost—the premilling steaming forces nutrients back into the endosperm or heart of the rice grain. Parboiled rice, also called converted, keeps longer than other rice, and sometimes requires a little more cooking time. Do not confuse it with instant or precooked rice.

POPCORN-STYLE RICE

See Aromatic Rice.

SHORT-GRAIN RICE (11)

Short-grain rice is shorter and plumper than medium-grain, and sometimes appears nearly round. White or brown, short-grain rice is very high in the starch *amylopectin* and when cooked, becomes sticky and soft. In this country, short-grain rice is most often available as brown rice from natural food stores. Short-grain white rice is used throughout Asia, but it is not exported to this country.

SPANISH- OR LATIN-STYLE MEDIUM-GRAIN RICE (7, 8)

Since many Spanish and Central and South American dishes use medium-grain white rice, it is often sold under labels that reflect this heritage. Valencia is a specialty rice from Spain used most often in paella.

STICKY, GLUTINOUS, WAXY, OR SWEET RICE (11)

This starchy rice, which is almost completely composed of *amylopectin*, is not actually sweet but is used throughout Asia in sweets and desserts. The rice is very short and stubby and sticks together when cooked; it may be either white or brown, and should not be replaced with another kind of rice. The kind of sticky rice grown in the U.S. is a type of short-grain, while in Asia a long-grain sticky rice is also grown.

SUSHI RICE (10)

See Medium-Grain Rice.

TEXMATI RICE (6)

A brand name for a hybrid of aromatics and domestic long-grain rice, it is similar to basmati in flavor and texture.

WILD RICE (14)

This is not a true rice, but an aquatic grass seed with a long, dark brown kernel, which requires long cooking similar to brown rice. The rice has a rich, nutty, earthy flavor with a chewy texture. Traditionally wild rice is harvested by hand, a process that makes it very expensive.

Less expensive cultivated "wild" rice is planted in paddies and harvested by machine. It takes about 3 pounds of the seed to yield 1 pound of good-quality wild rice. When cooked, however, the grain swells to three times its size. Blends are less expensive than premium wild rice.

RICE PRODUCTS

BROWN RICE SYRUP

A mild sweetener, also called rice malt, brown rice syrup is made from fermented rice. It is easily digestible and highly nutritious since it is made from the whole rice grain: the hull, bran, and kernel (germ). Use it as you would any sweetener or in baking.

RICE BRAN

Bran, the outer layer of the kernel, is high in fiber and some essential B vitamins. Rice bran is perishable and should be refrigerated once it has been opened.

RICE CAKES

These light, airy, and crunchy compressed cakes are made from puffed rice and are favored by people on low-fat diets and as snacks.

RICE FLOUR

Milled from white or brown rice, rice flour contains no gluten and so does not behave similarly to wheat flour in baked goods. Combined with wheat flour, it produces densely textured baked goods with a slightly gritty texture.

RICE NOODLES

Rice noodles are made from rice flour and are commonly used in Chinese, Thai, and other Asian dishes. They may be thick and fat or small and slender; both cook very quickly when dropped in boiling water.

RICE PAPER

Rice paper is thin, dried sheets of dough made from rice flour. The paper must first be dampened before being used as wrappers in Southeast Asian dishes (somewhat akin to wonton wrappers).

RICE VINEGAR

Rice vinegar has a gentle yet tart flavor and is milder than other vinegars.

SAKE

Sake is Japanese rice wine, distilled from steamed rice. It may be dry or sweet.

PERFECT STEAMED RICE

IN THIS METHOD, VERY LITTLE LIQUID IS USED,
RESULTING IN GRAINS THAT ARE FIRMER THAN IF COOKED BY THE
PACKAGE METHOD, BUT BECOME LIGHTER AND DRIER WHEN
FLUFFED WITH A FORK. PREPARE LONG-GRAIN BROWN RICE IN THE
SAME WAY BUT ALLOW 40 MINUTES FOR COOKING.

In a heavy-bottomed medium-size saucepan with a tight-fitting lid, combine the rice and enough cold water or broth to cover by ½ to 1 inch. Add salt to taste (if using canned broth, you may not need salt). Bring to a boil over high heat, stir, and tightly cover. Reduce the heat to very low and cook for 13 to 15 minutes, or until the rice is tender but firm, and all the liquid has been absorbed. Let the rice stand, covered for 3 to 4 minutes. Fluff the rice with a fork before serving.

1 ½ cups long- or medium-grain white rice

Cold water or broth

Salt to taste

PERFECT BAKED RICE

MAKES ABOUT 5 1/2 CUPS

RICE BAKED IN THE OVEN RUNS LESS CHANCE
OF SCORCHING THAN RICE COOKED ON THE STOVE TOP, AND
IS LIGHT AND FLUFFY AND TENDS TO BE A LITTLE
CREAMIER THAN STEAMED OR BAKED RICE. LONG-GRAIN BROWN
RICE WILL TAKE ABOUT 40 MINUTES TO BAKE.

1½ cups long- or medium-grain
    white rice

3 cups water or broth

Salt to taste

Preheat the oven to 400°F.

In a 1½-quart flameproof baking dish, combine the rice, water or broth, and salt to taste (if using canned broth, you may not need salt). Bring to a boil over high heat, stir, and cover tightly. Transfer the dish to the oven and bake for about 15 minutes, or until the rice is tender and all the liquid has been absorbed. Let the rice stand, covered, for 3 to 4 minutes. Fluff the rice with a fork before serving.

PERFECT BOILED RICE

MAKES ABOUT 5 1/2 CUPS

THIS METHOD MAY BE UNFAMILIAR, BUT IT IS A
SIMPLE, FOOLPROOF WAY TO COOK RICE SO THAT THE GRAINS
ARE LIGHT AND FLUFFY—IDEAL FOR RICE SALADS. LIKE
PASTA, COOKED RICE SHOULD BE AL DENTE, FIRM BUT TENDER.
ALLOW 40 MINUTES FOR LONG-GRAIN BROWN RICE.

In a large stockpot, bring the water or broth to a boil, then stir in the salt to taste (if using canned broth, you may not need salt). Sprinkle the rice over the water gradually so that the water does not stop boiling. Lower the heat to medium-low and cook for about 15 minutes, or until the rice is tender but still firm. Drain immediately in a medium-fine mesh sieve.

2 quarts water or broth
or a combination

Salt to taste

1½ cups long- or medium-grain
white rice

PERFECT MICROWAVED RICE

EVEN IF IT DOESN'T SAVE TIME, THE MICROWAVE IS AN
EXCELLENT WAY TO COOK RICE. THERE IS LITTLE RISK OF SCORCHING,
AND CHANCES ARE, THE RICE WILL BE PERFECT EVEN IF THE
LIQUID BOILS OVER ONTO THE TRAY. LONG-GRAIN BROWN RICE SHOULD
BE COOKED AT MEDIUM POWER FOR ABOUT 35 MINUTES.

1½ cups long- or medium-grain
   white rice

3 cups water or broth

Salt to taste

In a microwave-safe 1½-quart baking dish, stir together the rice, water or broth, and salt to taste (if using canned broth, you may not need salt). Cover tightly and microwave on High (100 percent) power for about 5 minutes, or until the liquid is boiling. Carefully uncover and stir the rice. Recover and microwave on Medium (50 percent) power for about 18 minutes, or until the rice is tender and all the liquid has been absorbed. Let the rice stand, covered, for 3 to 4 minutes. Fluff the rice with a fork before serving.

PERFECT WILD RICE

MAKES ABOUT 6 CUPS

WILD RICE IS NOT ACTUALLY RICE BUT A GRASS.
UNLIKE TRUE RICES, IT DOES NOT ABSORB ALL THE COOKING
LIQUID; AND IT PERMEATES A DISH WITH ITS OWN
FLAVORS. WILD RICE SHOULD BE RINSED AND WILL REQUIRE
A LONGER COOKING TIME THAN WHITE RICE.

P lace the rice in a fine-mesh strainer and rinse under cold running water. When the water runs clear, drain the rice.

In a heavy-bottomed, medium-size saucepan, bring the water or broth to a boil over high heat. Stir in the rice and add salt to taste. Return to a boil, stir, and cover. Reduce the heat to low and cook for about 40 minutes, or until the rice is tender and the outer hulls crack to expose the white interiors. Remove the rice from the heat and let stand, covered, for about 10 minutes. Drain.

1 ½ cups wild rice
4 ½ cups water or broth
Salt to taste

PORK & SHRIMP PEARL BALLS WITH SPICY SOY DIPPING SAUCE

SERVES 4 (ABOUT 20 SHRIMP BALLS)

A LUSTROUS COATING OF STEAMED STICKY RICE GIVES
THESE JUICY PORK AND SHRIMP BALLS A PEARL-LIKE QUALITY. THE
BALLS CAN BE PREPARED UP TO 24 HOURS AHEAD,
REFRIGERATED, AND THEN RE-STEAMED FOR ABOUT 10 MINUTES TO
REHEAT. SERVE AS AN HORS D'OEUVRE OR MAIN COURSE.

PEARL BALLS

½ cup sticky rice (also known as
glutinous or sweet rice)

4 ounces medium-size shrimp,
peeled & deveined

12 ounces ground pork

¼ cup minced drained & rinsed
water chestnuts

1 tablespoon dry sherry

1 tablespoon soy sauce

1 tablespoon cornstarch

1 green onion, minced

1 teaspoon coarsely grated
peeled fresh ginger

½ teaspoon sugar

¼ teaspoon salt

¼ teaspoon freshly ground
black pepper

Romaine leaves, for steaming

SPICY SOY DIPPING SAUCE

¼ cup soy sauce

2 tablespoons rice vinegar

2 tablespoons thinly sliced
green onion

¼ to ½ teaspoon hot chili
sesame oil

Prepare the pearl balls: In a medium-size bowl, combine the rice with hot water to cover by 1 inch. Let stand for 1 to 2 hours. Drain and return the rice to the bowl.

In a food processor fitted with the metal blade, process the shrimp to a paste. Scrape the paste into a bowl. Add the pork, water chestnuts, sherry, soy sauce, cornstarch, green onion, ginger, sugar, salt, and pepper, and mix well.

With moistened hands, roll about 1 tablespoon of the shrimp mixture into a ball, and then roll in the rice to coat. Transfer to a waxed-paper-lined baking sheet. Continue with the remaining mixture and rice; you should have about 20 balls.

Line 2 tiers of a stackable bamboo steamer with romaine leaves and place the rice balls on the lettuce. Stack the tiers and place over a large pot of boiling water. Cover the steamer and steam over medium heat for about 30 minutes, or until the balls are cooked through; test for doneness by cutting open one of the balls. You may have to add more hot water to the pot from time to time.

Meanwhile, prepare the dipping sauce: In a small bowl, stir together all the ingredients. Divide among 4 small bowls. Place 5 pearl balls on each plate. Serve immediately with the dipping sauce.

AVGOLEMONO SOUP
WITH CHICKEN

SERVES 6 TO 8

A TRADITIONAL PART OF GREEK COOKING,

AVGOLEMONO IS A TART, REFRESHING SAUCE MADE

FROM EGGS AND LEMON THAT IS WHISKED

INTO SOUPS JUST BEFORE SERVING—ANY SOONER AND

THE RESULT WOULD BE SCRAMBLED EGGS.

In a large nonreactive skillet, bring 3 cups of the broth to a boil over high heat. Reduce the heat, add the chicken and half the lemon zest, cover, and simmer for about 15 minutes, or until the chicken is just tender and no longer pink in the center. Remove the chicken from the broth and set aside to cool. Transfer the broth to a large nonreactive saucepan.

Add the remaining 3 cups broth to the saucepan and bring to a boil. Add the rice, reduce the heat, and simmer, uncovered, for about 15 minutes, or until the rice is nearly tender. Meanwhile, slice the chicken into 1- by ¼-inch strips.

Add the chicken to the soup and cook for about 5 minutes longer, or until the rice is tender. Remove from the heat.

In a small bowl, whisk together the lemon juice, egg yolks, and the remaining lemon zest. Whisk the egg mixture into the soup until the soup becomes cloudy. Stir in the mint, oregano, parsley, and pepper. Serve immediately, with a dollop of yogurt on each serving if desired.

6 cups chicken broth

2 boneless skinless chicken breast halves (about 5 ounces each)

Grated zest of ½ lemon

⅔ cup long-grain white rice

¼ cup fresh lemon juice

3 large egg yolks

1 tablespoon chopped fresh mint or 1 teaspoon dried

1 tablespoon chopped fresh oregano or 1 teaspoon dried

1 tablespoon chopped fresh flat-leaf parsley

1 teaspoon freshly ground black pepper

Plain low-fat yogurt, for garnish (optional)

VARIATION

• *Avgolemono Soup with Lamb:* Substitute 3 cups of lamb broth for the chicken broth. Omit the chicken and add 1 cup of cubed cooked lamb to the soup 3 to 4 minutes before the rice is tender.

INDONESIAN RICE SALAD WITH DRIED FRUITS & NUTS

SERVES 6

THE SWEET-TARTNESS OF THE DRIED FRUIT AND
THE FLAVORS OF THE CUMIN, CORIANDER, GARLIC, AND LEMON
SHINE THROUGH IN THIS SIMPLE RICE SALAD.
THIS IS WONDERFUL WITH GRILLED MEATS AND FISH, OR IT CAN
STAND ALONE, ACCOMPANIED BY A GREEN SALAD.

Prepare the dressing: In a small bowl, whisk together the lemon zest, lemon juice, vinegar, garlic, ginger, cumin, coriander, cayenne, and honey. Slowly whisk in the oil until thoroughly incorporated. Season with the salt and pepper.

Meanwhile, prepare the salad: Cook the rice following the basic method for boiled long-grain brown rice (p. 13) or according to the package directions. Let cool. In a small bowl, cover the sun-dried tomatoes with warm water and let stand for 30 minutes, or until softened. Drain and chop.

In a medium-size bowl, mix together the cooked rice, apricots, sun-dried tomatoes, bell pepper, green onions, cucumber, and nuts. Add the dressing and toss gently to mix well. Cover and refrigerate up to 1 hour.

Serve at room temperature, garnished with the cilantro and lemon zest.

DRESSING

Grated zest of 1 lemon, plus
    additional for garnish

¼ cup fresh lemon juice

1½ tablespoons tarragon vinegar

1 garlic clove, minced

1 teaspoon minced peeled
    fresh ginger

½ teaspoon ground cumin

½ teaspoon ground coriander

¼ teaspoon cayenne

2 tablespoons honey

¼ cup peanut oil

¼ teaspoon salt

¼ teaspoon freshly ground
    black pepper

1½ cups long-grain brown rice

¼ cup sun-dried tomatoes
    (not oil-packed)

½ cup chopped dried apricots

¼ cup diced red bell pepper

3 green onions, chopped

½ cup diced seeded cucumber

½ cup coarsely chopped mixed
    unsalted peanuts & cashews

1 tablespoon chopped fresh
    cilantro, for garnish

ASIAN RICE SALAD WITH GINGER SNOW PEAS & MUSHROOMS

SERVES 6

THIS CHILLED SALAD USES MEDIUM-GRAIN
ASIAN RICE BECAUSE ITS STARCHINESS ALLOWS THE
DRESSING TO COAT IT MORE THOROUGHLY.
THE DRESSING CAN BE MADE SEVERAL HOURS AHEAD
AND REFRIGERATED.

SALAD

1 cup dried oyster mushrooms
(about ¾ ounce)

1½ cups medium-grain white rice,
preferably Asian-style

1 tablespoon oriental sesame oil

1½ teaspoons olive oil

1 teaspoon grated peeled
fresh ginger

1 garlic clove, minced

¼ teaspoon salt

¼ teaspoon freshly ground
black pepper

¼ teaspoon hot pepper flakes

1½ teaspoons rice vinegar

2 tablespoons soy sauce

1 medium-size red bell pepper,
cored, seeded & diced

3 green onions, chopped

1 cup snow peas, blanched & sliced

½ cup canned water chestnuts,
drained, rinsed & cut in half

½ cup canned sliced bamboo
shoots, drained & rinsed

Prepare the salad: In a small bowl, combine the mushrooms with hot water to cover and let stand for about 15 minutes, or until softened. Drain the mushrooms in a sieve lined with a double thickness of cheesecloth or dampened paper towels placed over a bowl. Reserve 2 tablespoons of the soaking liquid, and refrigerate any remaining liquid for a soup, stew, or sauce. Rinse the mushrooms to remove any grit.

Meanwhile, cook the rice following the basic method for boiled rice (p. 13) or according to the package directions. Let cool.

In a small nonreactive skillet, heat the sesame oil and olive oil over medium-high heat. Add the ginger and garlic and cook, stirring, for about 1 minute, or until aromatic. Add the mushrooms, salt, pepper, and hot pepper flakes and cook, stirring frequently, for 3 to 4 minutes, or until the mushrooms absorb the oil and color slightly. Transfer the mushrooms to a plate.

Add the reserved 2 tablespoons mushroom soaking liquid, the vinegar, and soy sauce to the skillet and cook, scraping up any browned bits from the bottom of the pan, for 1 to 2 minutes. Return the mushrooms to the skillet, stir, and remove from the heat. Let cool.

Spoon the rice into a serving bowl. Add the mushrooms, bell pepper, green onions, snow peas, water chestnuts, and bamboo shoots and mix well.

Prepare the dressing: In a small bowl, combine the lemon juice, vinegar, ginger, and garlic. Gradually whisk in the oriental sesame oil.

Add the dressing to the rice salad and toss to coat. Cover and refrigerate up to 1 hour. Serve slightly chilled.

DRESSING

¼ cup plus 2 tablespoons fresh lemon juice

2 tablespoons rice vinegar

1 teaspoon grated peeled fresh ginger

1 garlic clove, minced

2 tablespoons oriental sesame oil

ITALIAN SEAFOOD RICE SALAD WITH LEMON-BASIL VINAIGRETTE

SERVES 6

NEARLY EVERY RESTAURANT ALONG THE PICTURESQUE
LIGURIAN COAST OF ITALY OFFERS THIS SEAFOOD SALAD, RICH
WITH SHRIMP, SCALLOPS, AND SQUID—THE CATCH
OF THE DAY. BECAUSE OF THE DELICACY OF THE FLAVORS,
THIS SALAD IS ALWAYS MADE FRESH.

2 cups Arborio or other
    medium-grain Italian rice

LEMON-BASIL VINAIGRETTE

¼ cup fresh lemon juice

1 small garlic clove, pressed

½ teaspoon salt

¼ teaspoon hot pepper flakes

½ cup chopped fresh basil

¾ cup olive oil

8 ounces medium-size shrimp
    in the shell

8 ounces sea scallops, halved
    or quartered if large

8 ounces cleaned squid (calamari),
    cut into ¼-inch-thick rings

Sprigs of fresh basil, for garnish
    (optional)

Cook the rice following the basic method for steamed rice (p. 11) or boiled rice (p. 13) or according to the package directions. Let cool, cover, and set aside.

Prepare the vinaigrette: In a small bowl, whisk together the lemon juice, garlic, salt, hot pepper flakes, and basil. Gradually whisk in the oil until well incorporated. Cover and set aside.

Bring a large saucepan of lightly salted water to a boil over high heat. Add the shrimp and cook for 2 to 3 minutes, or until pink and firm. Using a skimmer, transfer the shrimp to a colander and cool under cold running water. Drain and set aside.

Add the scallops to the boiling water and cook for about 1 minute, or until opaque. Using a skimmer, transfer to a colander and cool under cold running water. Drain and transfer to a bowl.

Add the squid to the boiling water and cook for about 30 seconds, or until barely firm and opaque. Drain and rinse under cold running water. Drain and add to the scallops.

Peel the shrimp and add them to the bowl with the scallops and squid. Cover and refrigerate until ready to serve.

Combine the rice and seafood. Pour the dressing over the salad, and toss well, and serve, garnished with fresh basil, if desired.

VEGETARIAN SUSHI RICE BOWL

SERVES 6

THE JAPANESE OFTEN EAT *CHIRASHI-ZUSHI*—
VINEGARED SUSHI RICE SIMPLY SPOONED INTO A BOWL AND
TOPPED WITH TRADITIONAL SUSHI INGREDIENTS.
IT IS A DELIGHTFUL WAY TO EXPERIENCE THE FLAVORS OF
SUSHI WITHOUT THE FUSS OF SHAPING IT.

3⅓ cups medium-grain rice,
  preferably Asian-style
  (sushi rice)

¼ cup plus 2 tablespoons
  rice vinegar

2 tablespoons plus
  2 teaspoons sugar

½ teaspoon salt

6 dried shiitake or other
  dried dark mushrooms

1 tablespoon soy sauce

1 tablespoon sake or dry sherry

2 large eggs, lightly beaten

1 cup sliced (¼-inch pieces)
  green beans

1 sheet nori (laver seaweed)

1 medium-size carrot, julienned

2 green onions, thinly sliced

Place the rice in a fine-meshed sieve and rinse under cold running water until the water runs clear. Drain well.

In a medium-size saucepan, bring 4 cups water to a boil over high heat. Add the rice, cover, and cook for 5 minutes. Reduce the heat to low and cook for about 5 minutes longer, or until the rice is tender and all the liquid has been absorbed. Remove from the heat and let stand, covered, for 10 minutes.

In a small nonreactive saucepan, bring the rice vinegar, 2 tablespoons plus 1 teaspoon of the sugar, and the salt to a simmer over low heat, stirring to dissolve the sugar. Remove from the heat.

Transfer the rice to a large nonreactive bowl. Cool the rice using a fan or a hair dryer set on cool; at the same time, cut through the rice, using a wooden spoon, and toss it with the vinegar mixture. (This is done more easily with 2 people.) When the rice reaches room temperature, cover with a damp kitchen towel and set aside. (Do not refrigerate.)

In a small bowl, combine the dried mushrooms with hot water to cover. Let stand for 30 minutes, or until softened. Drain the mushrooms, rinse to remove any grit, and squeeze out the excess water. Cut the mushrooms into pieces.

In a small nonreactive saucepan, bring the soy sauce, sake or sherry, and remaining 1 teaspoon

sugar to a simmer over low heat, stirring to dissolve the sugar. Add the mushrooms and cook for about 1 minute, or until they absorb the liquid. Transfer to a plate to cool.

Heat a medium-size nonstick skillet over medium heat. Add half the eggs and tilt the skillet to coat the bottom evenly. Cook for about 30 seconds, or until the egg is set and the edges are dry. Using a rubber spatula, loosen the egg from the pan and then, using your fingers, flip the egg over. Cook for about 15 seconds, or until the underside is dry. Transfer to a plate to cool completely. Repeat with the remaining egg.

Roll each egg sheet into a cylinder and cut into ¼-inch-wide slices. Unroll and set aside.

Bring a small saucepan of lightly salted water to a boil over high heat. Add the green beans and cook for 1 to 2 minutes, or until crisp-tender. Drain, rinse under cold running water, and drain again. Set aside.

Grasp the nori with a pair of tongs and, holding it shiny side down, pass it 2 or 3 times over a hot electric or gas burner until lightly crisped and fragrant. Take care not to scorch the nori. Crumble into a small bowl.

To serve, spoon the rice into shallow soup bowls. Top with the mushrooms, eggs, green beans, carrot, green onions, and nori. Serve immediately.

ASPARAGUS & PROSCIUTTO RISOTTO

SERVES 4

RISOTTO IS A NORTHERN ITALIAN CLASSIC THAT CAN BE FLAVORED
WITH ANYTHING FROM SHELLFISH TO BEEF MARROW. IT IS ESSENTIAL TO USE
ONE OF THE ITALIAN MEDIUM-GRAIN RICES, SUCH AS ARBORIO OR
CARNAROLI, AS THEY CONTAIN THE STARCH COMPONENT NECESSARY FOR
RISOTTO'S CHARACTERISTIC CREAMINESS.

1 pound thin asparagus spears

6 cups veal or chicken broth or canned low-sodium chicken broth, or more as needed

1 cup dry white wine

4 tablespoons (½ stick) unsalted butter, at room temperature

⅔ cup finely chopped onion

2 ounces sliced prosciutto, coarsely chopped

2 cups Arborio or other medium-grain Italian rice

¾ cup freshly grated Parmesan cheese

¼ teaspoon salt, or to taste

⅛ teaspoon freshly ground black pepper

Snap the thick bottom ends off the asparagus and coarsely chop them. Cut the spears into ½-inch lengths and set aside.

In a medium-size nonreactive saucepan, combine the stock and wine and bring to a boil over high heat. Add the chopped asparagus ends, return to a boil, and cook for about 15 minutes, or until the asparagus is tender. Strain the stock through a colander set over a bowl, pressing on the asparagus to extract the liquid. Discard the asparagus.

Return the stock to the saucepan and bring to a boil over medium-high heat. Add the reserved asparagus and cook for about 2 minutes, or until crisp-tender. Using a slotted spoon, transfer to a bowl and set aside. Reduce the heat to keep the stock at a bare simmer.

In a heavy large nonreactive saucepan, melt 2 tablespoons of the butter over medium heat. Add the onion and prosciutto and cook, stirring often, for about 5 minutes, or until the onion is golden and softened. Add the rice and stir for 1 minute. Ladle about ¾ cup of the hot stock into the saucepan, reduce the heat to low, and stir for about 3 minutes, or until the rice has absorbed the liquid, adjusting the heat as necessary so the mixture maintains a gentle boil. Ladle another ¾ cup of hot stock into the pan and stir until the rice has

absorbed the liquid. Continue this procedure until the rice is al dente, tender with a slight "bite" in the center. The entire process will take 20 to 30 minutes, and there may be some broth left over; if all the stock is used before the rice is tender, add additional broth or hot water. During the last 2 minutes of cooking, add the asparagus spears. If necessary, stir in a final ¾ cup of stock to give the risotto a spoonable, creamy consistency. Be flexible with your timing and the amount of broth: The important thing is the correct creamy consistency.

Remove from the heat and stir in the Parmesan and the remaining 2 tablespoons butter. Season with the salt and pepper and serve hot.

VARIATIONS

- *Saffron Risotto:* Omit the asparagus and prosciutto. During the last 2 minutes of cooking, stir in ½ teaspoon crumbled saffron threads soaked in 2 tablespoons of the hot broth.
- *Venetian Risotto with Peas:* Omit the asparagus. Cook 2 cups fresh peas (from 2 pounds pea pods) in the simmering broth for the risotto for about 2 minutes, or until tender. Using a slotted spoon, remove the peas from the broth and set aside. (You may also use thawed frozen peas.) During the last 2 minutes of cooking, stir in the peas.

Asparagus & Prosciutto Risotto (overleaf)

SPINACH & RICE TIMBALE

SERVES 8 TO 10

THIS MOLDED RICE DISH IS BAKED IN A
SPRINGFORM PAN AND SERVED WITH A TRADITIONAL
TOMATO SAUCE. SERVE IT WITH A
COLD VEGETABLE SALAD, SUCH AS STRING BEANS
IN OIL AND VINEGAR.

TIMBALE

1 tablespoon unsalted butter, at
    room temperature

1½ teaspoons finely ground dried
    bread crumbs

⅔ cup long-grain white rice

1 tablespoon olive oil

12 ounces sweet Italian sausage,
    casings removed

1 medium-size onion, finely
    chopped

1 medium-size red bell pepper,
    cored, seeded & chopped

1 garlic clove, minced

2 (10-ounce) packages frozen
    chopped spinach, thawed &
    squeezed dry, or 2 pounds
    fresh spinach, stems removed

1 (15-ounce) container part-skim
    ricotta cheese

½ cup freshly grated
    Parmesan cheese

½ cup chopped fresh basil

5 large eggs, well beaten

¼ teaspoon salt, or to taste

¼ teaspoon hot pepper flakes

Prepare the timbale: Preheat the oven to 350°F. Grease a 9-inch springform pan with the butter and sprinkle the sides and bottom with the bread crumbs, tilting the pan to coat it.

Cook the rice following the basic method for boiled rice (p. 13) or according to the package directions. Set aside.

In a large nonreactive skillet, heat the oil over medium heat. Add the sausage, onion, bell pepper, and garlic, and cook, breaking up the sausage with a wooden spoon, for about 7 minutes, or until the sausage is no longer pink. With a slotted spoon, remove the sausage and vegetables to a bowl and discard all but 1 tablespoon fat.

If using fresh spinach, place the wet spinach in a large saucepan, cover, and cook 6 to 7 minutes, or until wilted. Drain, rinse under cold running water, and squeeze dry. Coarsely chop.

Stir the rice, spinach, ricotta, Parmesan, and basil into the sausage mixture. Add the eggs and mix well. Season with the salt and hot pepper flakes. (The sausage and Parmesan are salty: add salt judiciously.) Transfer the mixture to the prepared springform pan and smooth the top.

Bake for about 1¼ hours, or until a knife inserted in the center comes out clean. Transfer the timbale to a wire rack to cool for 10 minutes.

Meanwhile, prepare the sauce: In a medium-size nonreactive saucepan, heat the reserved tablespoon of fat or the olive oil over medium heat. Add the onion and cook, stirring frequently, for about 5 minutes, or until softened. Add the garlic and cook for 30 seconds, or until aromatic. Add the tomatoes and bring to a boil. Reduce the heat to low and simmer for about 30 minutes, or until the sauce has thickened. Stir in the basil, salt, and hot pepper flakes and simmer for 5 minutes longer.

Pour the sauce into a food processor fitted with the metal blade. Process until the sauce is a slightly chunky purée. Return the sauce to the saucepan and cover to keep warm.

Cut the timbale into wedges and serve with the warm sauce, garnished with basil sprigs, if desired.

TOMATO-BASIL SAUCE

1 tablespoon olive oil (optional)

1 medium-size onion, chopped

1 garlic clove, minced

2 pounds ripe plum tomatoes, peeled, cored, seeded & chopped, or 1 (28-ounce) can peeled whole tomatoes in juice, undrained & chopped

¼ cup chopped fresh basil

¼ teaspoon salt, or to taste

⅛ teaspoon hot pepper flakes

Sprigs of fresh basil, for garnish (optional)

CARIBBEAN BLACK BEANS & RICE

SERVES 4

BLACK BEANS AND RICE, SERVED AS A

SIDE DISH THROUGHOUT THE CARIBBEAN, CENTRAL AND

SOUTH AMERICA, AND SPAIN, ALSO MAKES

A SATISFYING AND FILLING MAIN COURSE, SERVED WITH

A CRISP GREEN SALAD.

1⅓ cups dried black beans, picked over & rinsed

1 tablespoon lard or olive oil

2 ounces smoked ham, cut into ¼-inch cubes

1 small onion, chopped

½ cup chopped green bell pepper

1 garlic clove, minced

1 cup chopped peeled cored & seeded ripe plum tomatoes, or 1 (15-ounce) can peeled whole tomatoes in juice, drained & chopped

1¾ cups beef broth

1 teaspoon dried oregano

1 bay leaf

¼ teaspoon freshly ground black pepper

1½ cups medium-grain white rice

1 tablespoon red wine vinegar

Sprigs of fresh oregano, for garnish (optional)

In a medium-size nonreactive saucepan, combine the beans and water to cover by 1 inch. Bring to a boil over high heat and cook for 2 minutes. Remove from the heat, cover, and let stand for 1 hour. Drain, and set aside. Wipe the saucepan dry.

In the same saucepan, heat the lard or oil over medium heat. Add the ham, onion, bell pepper, and garlic and cook, stirring often, for about 5 minutes, or until the onion is softened. Add the tomatoes and cook for about 3 minutes, or until the juices have evaporated. Add the beans, broth, 1 cup water, oregano, bay leaf, and black pepper. Bring to a boil over high heat. Reduce the heat to low, partially cover, and simmer for about 45 minutes, or until the beans are just tender. Drain, reserving the cooking liquid. Set the beans aside. Discard the bay leaf.

Cook the rice following the basic method for steamed rice (p. 11) or according to the package directions.

Meanwhile, return the bean cooking liquid to the saucepan and stir in the vinegar. Bring to a boil over high heat and cook until reduced to about 1 cup. Stir in the beans and cook for 1 minute, or until heated through.

Mound the hot rice in a large shallow serving bowl, making a well in the center, and pour the beans into the well. Serve immediately, garnished with oregano sprigs, if desired.

MUSHROOMS & RICE
ENCHILADAS WITH CHEDDAR

SERVES 6

THE MUSHROOMS PROVIDE HEARTY FLAVOR AND
MEATY TEXTURE TO THESE ENCHILADAS, MAKING THEM A SATISFYING
MEATLESS MAIN COURSE. ORDINARY WHITE BUTTON
MUSHROOMS ARE FINE, BUT IF YOU CAN FIND THEM, USE CREMINI
OR SHIITAKE FOR A DEEPER, BOLDER FLAVOR.

FILLING

½ cup long-grain white
   or brown rice

1 tablespoon unsalted butter

1 medium-size onion, chopped

2 medium-size red bell peppers,
   cored, seeded & chopped

1 jalapeño or hot chile pepper,
   seeded & minced

2 garlic cloves, minced

1 pound mushrooms, stemmed

4 ounces sharp cheddar cheese,
   cut into ½-inch dice

2 large eggs, lightly beaten

½ teaspoon salt

¼ teaspoon freshly ground
   black pepper

SAUCE

1 (28-ounce) can peeled tomatoes
   in thick purée

1 (8-ounce) can tomato sauce

1 small onion, quartered

2 garlic cloves, peeled

2 tablespoons chili powder,
   or to taste

2 tablespoons unbleached
   all-purpose flour

1 teaspoon ground cumin

Prepare the filling: Cook the rice following the basic method for steamed rice (p. 11), or according to the package directions. (Or use 1¾ cups leftover cooked rice.) Let cool.

In a large skillet, melt the butter over medium heat. Add the onion, bell peppers, jalapeño, and garlic and cook, stirring frequently, for about 5 minutes, or until the onion is softened. Add the mushrooms and cook for about 7 minutes, or until the liquid has evaporated and the mushrooms are lightly browned. Transfer to a medium-size bowl and stir in the rice, cheddar, eggs, salt, and pepper.

Prepare the sauce: In a blender, combine the tomatoes with the purée, the tomato sauce, onion, garlic, chili powder, flour, cumin, and oregano and process to a smooth purée. Pour into a bowl.

In a large skillet, heat the oil over medium heat. Add the puréed tomato mixture and bring to a simmer. Reduce the heat to low and simmer, partially covered, for 3 minutes. Remove from the heat and set aside.

Preheat the oven to 350°F. Lightly grease a 15- by 10-inch baking dish.

Assemble the enchiladas: Spread a thin layer of tomato sauce in the baking dish. Lightly grease a large non-stick skillet and place over medium heat. Lay a tortilla in the skillet and heat for 30 seconds,

or until softened. Using tongs, dip the tortilla in the tomato sauce, turning to coat it on both sides, and transfer to a plate. Spoon about ⅓ cup of the filling down the center of the tortilla. Roll the tortilla up around the filling and lay the enchilada, seam side down, in the baking dish. Continue making enchiladas with the remaining ingredients. Pour the remaining sauce over the enchiladas and sprinkle with the shredded cheddar.

Cover the dish with foil and bake for 30 minutes. Remove the foil and bake for about 10 minutes longer, or until the sauce is bubbling and the enchiladas are heated through. Serve immediately.

1 teaspoon dried oregano

1 tablespoon olive oil

12 corn tortillas

1 cup shredded sharp cheddar cheese

*Mushroom & Rice Enchiladas
with Cheddar (overleaf)*

ARROZ CON POLLO

SERVES 6

THE STRAIGHTFORWARD RECIPE FOR THIS CLASSIC
LATIN DISH IS ADAPTED FROM ONE PROVIDED BY ADELA STEWART,
A NATIVE OF COSTA RICA. IT'S A SIMPLE RENDITION
OF THE ULTIMATE COMFORT FOOD: CHICKEN AND RICE. ADELA
PREFERS MEDIUM-GRAIN RICE—AND LOTS OF GARLIC!

1 (3½ pound) chicken, cut
    into 8 pieces

½ teaspoon salt

¼ teaspoon freshly ground
    black pepper

2 tablespoons olive oil

1 large onion, thinly sliced

1 medium-size red bell pepper,
    cored, seeded & thinly sliced

3 large garlic cloves, minced

2 medium-size carrots, sliced

2 celery stalks, sliced

3 cups chicken broth

Salt & freshly ground black
    pepper to taste

2 cups medium-grain white rice,
    preferably Spanish-style

Pat the chicken dry and season with the salt and pepper. In a large skillet or Dutch oven, heat the oil over medium-high heat. Add the chicken, working in batches if necessary, and cook for 4 to 5 minutes per side, or until browned all over. Transfer the chicken to a plate and set aside.

Add the onion and bell pepper to the skillet and cook, stirring, for about 5 minutes, or until the onion softens. Add the garlic, carrots, and celery, and cook, stirring occasionally, for about 10 minutes, or until the carrots and celery are softened.

Add the broth and season to taste with salt and pepper. Return the chicken to the pan, partially cover, and simmer, stirring occasionally, for 25 minutes. Add the rice and simmer, partially covered, for about 25 minutes longer, or until the rice is tender and all the liquid has been absorbed. Spoon the rice and chicken onto a platter and serve.

CHICKEN BIRYANI

SERVES 6

FESTIVE OCCASIONS CALL FOR EXTRAVAGANT DISHES,

AND BIRYANI IS OFTEN GARNISHED WITH EDIBLE GOLD LEAF AND

SERVED AT WEDDINGS IN NORTHERN INDIA. THIS

VERSION, RICH WITH RAISINS, GINGER, AND YOGURT, MIMICS

THE GOLD LEAF WITH SAFFRON THREADS.

Prepare the marinade: In a blender, combine all the ingredients and process until smooth. Transfer to a nonreactive bowl and stir in the chicken. Cover and refrigerate for 2 to 6 hours.

In a 5-quart Dutch oven, heat the oil and butter over medium heat. Add the raisins and cook for 1 minute, or until plump. Transfer the raisins to a plate.

Add the onions to the pot and cook, stirring often, for about 10 minutes, or until golden brown. Transfer one third of the onions to the plate with the raisins. Add the cinnamon, cardamom, cloves, and bay leaves to the pot and cook, stirring, for 1 minute. Add the chicken and marinade. Bring to a boil and cook, stirring often, for 15 minutes, until the marinade has reduced by half.

Preheat the oven to 325°F. In a small saucepan, heat the milk until hot. Remove from the heat and stir in the saffron.

Bring a large pot of lightly salted water to a boil. Stir in the rice, return to a boil, and cook for 5 minutes. Drain. Stir the rice into the simmering chicken and drizzle the saffron-milk over. Cover and bake for about 30 minutes. Let stand, covered, for 5 minutes, or until the rice is tender. Transfer to a heated platter. Remove the bay leaves, cinnamon stick, and the cardamom pods. Top with the reserved onions and raisins, and serve.

MARINADE

1 cup plain low-fat yogurt

1 medium onion, coarsely chopped

¼ cup fresh lemon juice

1 tablespoon grated peeled
    fresh ginger

1 jalapeño or hot chile pepper,
    seeded & minced

2 garlic cloves, crushed

2 teaspoons Madras-style
    curry powder

1 teaspoon salt

6 skinless chicken breast halves, on
    the bone (about 6 ounces each)

2 tablespoons vegetable oil

2 tablespoons unsalted butter

¾ cup dark seedless raisins

2 large onions, halved lengthwise
    & thinly sliced crosswise

1 cinnamon stick

12 green cardamom pods, cracked

12 whole cloves

2 bay leaves

2 tablespoons milk

½ teaspoon crumbled
    saffron threads

2 cups basmati rice

TURKEY & SHRIMP JAMBALAYA

SERVES 6 TO 8

ESSENTIAL TO THE FLAVOR OF THIS BELOVED NEW ORLEANS
DISH IS A COMPLEX COMBINATION OF HOT AND SAVORY SPICES CALLED
CREOLE SEASONING. JAMBALAYA CALLS FOR LONG-GRAIN
RICE, WHICH IS WIDELY GROWN IN LOUISIANA, BECAUSE ITS GRAINS
REMAIN SEPARATE DURING COOKING.

In a 5-quart nonreactive Dutch oven or casserole, heat the oil over medium heat. Add the turkey or chicken and cook, stirring occasionally, for about 5 minutes, or until browned on all sides. Transfer to a plate and set aside.

Add the shrimp to the pot, adding more oil if necessary, and cook, turning once, for about 3 minutes, or until firm and pink. Transfer the shrimp to the plate and set aside.

In the same pot, melt the butter over medium heat. Add the ham, onion, bell pepper, celery, green onions, and garlic and cook, stirring often, for about 5 minutes, or until the onion is softened. Add the rice and Creole seasoning and stir for 1 minute. Add 2 cups water, the vegetable juice, and Worcestershire sauce, and bring to a boil. Reduce the heat to low, cover, and simmer for about 20 minutes, or until the rice is tender. Stir in the turkey and shrimp, remove from the heat, and cover. Let stand for about 5 minutes. Stir well, sprinkle with the parsley, and garnish with the reserved celery leaves, if desired. Serve immediately.

2 tablespoons vegetable oil,
  or more as necessary

1 pound boneless skinless
  turkey or chicken breasts,
  cut into 2- by 1-inch strips

1 pound medium-size shrimp,
  peeled & deveined

2 tablespoons unsalted butter

8 ounces thickly sliced smoked
  ham, cut into 1-inch pieces

1 medium-size onion, chopped

1 medium-size green bell pepper,
  cored, seeded & chopped

1 celery stalk with leaves,
  stalk chopped, leaves
  reserved for garnish (optional)

2 green onions, chopped

2 garlic cloves, minced

1½ cups long-grain white rice

2 teaspoons Creole seasoning

1½ cups tomato-vegetable juice

2 tablespoons Worcestershire sauce

2 tablespoons chopped fresh
  flat-leaf parsley

SAUSAGE GUMBO

SERVES 6 TO 8

A CLASSIC OF CAJUN AND CREOLE COOKING, GUMBO IS THICKENED
WITH EITHER FILÉ POWDER OR OKRA—WITHOUT ONE OR THE OTHER IT CAN'T
BE CALLED GUMBO. FILÉ, MADE FROM THE DRIED LEAVES OF
THE SASSAFRAS TREE, IS ADDED TO THE DISH AT THE VERY LAST MINUTE, OFF
THE HEAT, SINCE TOO MUCH HEAT CAN MAKE IT TOUGH AND STRINGY.

½ cup vegetable oil

½ cup unbleached
all-purpose flour

2 celery stalks with leaves, chopped

2 medium-size green bell peppers,
cored, seeded & chopped

1 medium-size onion, chopped

4 green onions, chopped

1 jalapeño, seeded & chopped

3 garlic cloves, minced

6 cups chicken broth

1 (35-ounce) can peeled whole
tomatoes in juice

¼ cup chopped fresh
flat-leaf parsley

2 bay leaves

1 teaspoon paprika

1 teaspoon dried thyme

1 teaspoon dried oregano

¼ teaspoon freshly ground
black pepper

1¼ pounds sweet or hot Italian
sausage or fresh chorizo
sausage, cut into 1-inch pieces

1½ cups long-grain white rice

1 generous tablespoon filé powder,
or more as needed

Chopped green onions, for garnish

In a 5- to 6-quart nonreactive Dutch oven or casserole, heat the oil over medium-high heat. Gradually whisk in the flour. Reduce the heat to medium and cook, whisking constantly, for 4 to 5 minutes, until the flour mixture, or roux, turns light brown; watch it closely and do not let it burn.

Add the celery, bell peppers, onion, green onions, and jalapeño, stirring to coat the vegetables with the roux. Cover and cook for about 5 minutes, or until the vegetables are softened. Stir in the garlic and cook for 1 minute longer. If necessary, add 1 to 2 tablespoons of the broth to the pan to keep the vegetables from sticking.

Add the tomatoes with their juice, the parsley, bay leaves, paprika, thyme, oregano, and black pepper. Stir in all the chicken broth and bring to a boil, breaking apart the tomatoes with a wooden spoon. Reduce the heat to low, partially cover, and simmer for 1 hour. The gumbo can be made a day ahead to this point, and kept refrigerated. It should be gently reheated to a simmer before finishing the recipe.

Meanwhile, in a medium-size nonreactive skillet, cook the sausage over medium-high heat, turning several times, for 5 to 7 minutes, or until browned. Drain in a colander and set aside.

Cook the rice following the basic method for steamed rice (p. 11) or boiled rice (p. 13) or according to the package directions. Cover the rice to keep warm.

Stir the sausage into the simmering soup. Remove the pot from the heat and stir in the filé powder until the soup's liquid thickens to the consistency of unbeaten egg whites. If desired, add more filé for a thicker soup.

Spoon the hot rice into warmed soup bowls. Ladle the gumbo over the rice. Garnish with chopped green onions and serve immediately.

VARIATION

- *Shrimp & Sausage Gumbo:* Shell and devein 8 ounces medium-size uncooked shrimp and add to the gumbo before adding the filé powder. Cook the gumbo for about 3 minutes, or until the shrimp are pink and firm, then add the filé powder and proceed as above.

CLASSIC PAELLA

S E R V E S   8

PAELLA HAS MANY INCARNATIONS BUT THE TRADITIONAL
SHELLFISH, PORK, AND CHICKEN VERSION IS THE MOST POPULAR. IT'S
WORTH THE EFFORT TO SEARCH OUT A REAL PAELLA PAN.
LACKING ONE, USE A 12-INCH SKILLET FOR THE INITIAL COOKING, AND
THEN BAKE IN TWO LIGHTLY OILED ROASTING PANS.

¼ cup fresh lemon juice

¼ cup plus 1 tablespoon olive oil

4 garlic cloves, 2 pressed, 2 minced

1 teaspoon paprika

¾ teaspoon salt

¼ teaspoon freshly ground
    black pepper

4 chicken breast halves on the bone
    (about 6 ounces each),
    cut in half crosswise

1 pound pork tenderloin, cut
    into 1-inch pieces

6 cups chicken broth

¾ cup dry white wine

½ teaspoon crumbled
    saffron threads

1 pound medium-size shrimp,
    peeled & deveined

8 ounces smoked chorizo, cut into
    ½-inch-thick rounds

1 medium-size onion, chopped

1 medium-size red bell pepper,
    cored, seeded & chopped

1 cup chopped drained
    canned tomatoes

⅓ cup chopped fresh
    flat-leaf parsley

3 cups medium-grain white rice,
    preferably Spanish-style

In a large bowl, combine the lemon juice, 2 tablespoons of the oil, the pressed garlic, paprika, ½ teaspoon of the salt, and the pepper. Add the chicken and pork and toss to coat well. Cover with plastic wrap and refrigerate for at least 3 hours, or up to 6 hours. Drain and discard the marinade.

In a medium-size saucepan, combine the broth, wine, saffron, and the remaining ¼ teaspoon salt. Bring to a boil over high heat. Remove from the heat and set aside.

Set a large paella pan (about 15 inches in diameter) over two burners. Add the remaining 3 tablespoons oil to the pan, tilting to coat, and heat over medium-high heat. Add the chicken and pork, working in batches if necessary, and cook for about 3 minutes per side, or until well browned. Transfer to a platter and set aside. Add the shrimp and cook, stirring frequently, for about 2 minutes, or until pink. Transfer to the platter. Reduce the heat to medium, add the chorizo, onion, and bell pepper, and cook, stirring often, for about 5 minutes, or until the onion is softened. Add the tomatoes and parsley and cook, stirring, for about 2 minutes, or until the tomato juices have evaporated.

(The paella can be prepared to this point about 2 hours ahead. Cover and refrigerate the meat and shrimp, the chorizo-tomato mixture, and the broth

separately. When ready to proceed, reheat the chorizo-tomato mixture and the broth mixture separately until both are hot.)

Preheat the oven to 350°F. Add the rice to the paella pan and stir until well coated. Pour in the broth and bring to a boil over medium heat, stirring frequently. Using a spoon, push the shrimp into the rice to partially cover and then add the chicken, pork, and artichokes. Scatter the mussels and clams over the top. Transfer the pan to the oven and cook, uncovered, for 20 to 25 minutes, or until most of the liquid has evaporated but the rice is still somewhat firm. Remove from the oven, discard any unopened shellfish. Cover with foil, and let stand in a warm place for about 10 minutes, or until the rice is tender. Serve immediately with lemon wedges.

1 (10-ounce) package thawed
  frozen artichoke hearts

12 mussels, beards removed
  & scrubbed

12 littleneck clams, scrubbed

Lemon wedges, for garnish

Classic Paella (overleaf)

CHINESE BEEF & VEGETABLES
ON SIZZLING RICE

SERVES 4 TO 6

WHEN THE BEEF AND VEGETABLES ARE SPOONED OVER
THE HOT RICE CRUST IN THIS RECIPE, THE DISH SIZZLES, CREATING AN
EXCITING AND DRAMATIC PRESENTATION. THE RICE CRUST
MUST BE ABSOLUTELY DRY BEFORE DEEP-FRYING—IF THE WEATHER IS
ESPECIALLY HUMID, DON'T EVEN ATTEMPT THIS DISH.

RICE CRUST

1 cup long-grain white rice

SIZZLING BEEF

2 cups chicken broth

2 tablespoons soy sauce

2 tablespoons tomato paste

2 tablespoons dry sherry

2 tablespoons rice vinegar

2 tablespoons sugar

½ teaspoon hot pepper flakes

2 tablespoons cornstarch

2 tablespoons vegetable
or peanut oil

2 teaspoons coarsely grated
peeled fresh ginger

2 garlic cloves, minced

12 ounces beef eye of round steak,
flank steak, or London broil,
partially frozen then cut
diagonally across the grain
into ¼-inch-thick slices

1 medium-size carrot, thickly cut
on the diagonal

1 medium-size celery stalk,
cut diagonally into
¼-inch-thick slices

Prepare the rice crust: In a large saucepan, cook the rice following the basic method for steamed rice (p. 11) or according to the package directions. When the rice is tender and all the liquid has been absorbed, uncover the pan and reduce the heat to as low as possible. Cook, checking frequently, for about 1 hour, or until the rice is golden brown in spots on the bottom. If the rice seems to be burning, set the pan on a flame tamer. If using a gas stove, shift the position of the pan several times to prevent scorching. Remove from the heat and let cool.

Run a sharp knife around the edge of the crust to release it. Invert the crust onto a plate. Let air-dry at room temperature for at least 8 hours, or overnight. If the crust is still not completely dry, slide it onto a baking sheet and bake it in a 200°F oven until bone-dry, up to 2 hours.

Prepare the sizzling beef: In a medium-size bowl, whisk together the broth, soy sauce, tomato paste, sherry, vinegar, sugar, and hot pepper flakes. Remove 2 tablespoons of the mixture to a little bowl and dissolve the cornstarch in it, then stir this mixture back into the sauce.

Heat a wok or large skillet over high heat until very hot. Add the oil and tilt the pan to coat it. Add the ginger and garlic and stir-fry for 30 seconds, or until aromatic. Add the beef and stir-fry for about 2 minutes, or until no longer pink. Add the carrot,

celery, bell pepper, snow peas, green onions, corn, and bamboo shoots and stir-fry for 1 minute. Add the sauce and bring to a simmer, stirring. Remove from the heat. The beef mixture can be prepared up to 1 hour ahead and then refrigerated, covered.

Preheat the oven to 350°F. Put a heavy rimmed baking sheet in the oven to heat.

Pour 2 inches of oil into a deep-fat fryer or large deep skillet and heat to 375°F. Break the rice crust into 6 equal wedges. Deep-fry the wedges, 1 or 2 at a time, for about 2 minutes, or until they are lightly browned and float to the surface. Drain on a paper-towel-lined platter. Let the oil return to 375°F before frying the next batch.

Bring the beef mixture to a boil. Meanwhile, place the fried crusts on the preheated baking sheet and bake for about 2 minutes.

Bring the hot baking sheet and skillet to the table. Carefully spoon the beef mixture over the rice. Serve immediately, garnished with fresh herbs.

1 medium-size red bell pepper, cored, seeded & cut lengthwise into ½-inch-wide strips

1 cup snow peas

2 green onions, thinly sliced

1 (15-ounce) can whole baby corn, drained & rinsed

1 cup sliced bamboo shoots, drained & rinsed

Vegetable oil, for deep-frying

Fresh basil or cilantro leaves, for garnish (optional)

SNAPPER PULAU WITH CILANTRO

SERVES 6

THIS BRACING INDIAN PILAF IS SEASONED
WITH A SPICE MIXTURE KNOWN AS GARAM MASALA
("WARM SPICES"). ONCE MADE, THE MIXTURE
CAN BE STORED FOR WEEKS AND ADDED TO SOUPS, STEWS
AND OTHER DISHES FOR A SPICY UNDERTONE.

GARAM MASALA

12 green cardamom pods

2 tablespoons coriander seeds

1 tablespoon cumin seeds

1½ teaspoons black peppercorns

¼ teaspoon whole cloves

¼ teaspoon grated nutmeg

3 tablespoons vegetable oil

1¼ pounds red snapper, scrod, or
    cod fillets, ¾ to 1 inch thick,
    cut into 1-inch pieces

2 tablespoons unsalted butter

1 large onion, halved lengthwise
    & thinly sliced crosswise

2 teaspoons grated peeled
    fresh ginger

1 jalapeño or hot chile pepper,
    seeded & minced

2 garlic cloves, minced

1 cinnamon stick

2 cups basmati rice

4 cups fish broth or 2 cups
    bottled clam juice mixed
    with 2 cups water

Prepare the garam masala: Heat a medium-size skillet over medium heat. Add the cardamom and toast, stirring often, for about 2 minutes, or until lightly browned and fragrant. Transfer to a plate to cool. Split the pods and remove the seeds, discarding the pods.

In the same skillet, toast the coriander seeds, cumin seeds, peppercorns, and cloves over medium heat, stirring often, for 2 to 3 minutes, or until lightly browned and fragrant. Transfer to the plate to cool.

In a spice grinder or with a mortar and pestle, combine the toasted spices and nutmeg and process or grind until finely ground. Reserve 1½ teaspoons of the garam masala and store the remainder in a tightly sealed glass jar in a cool, dark place.

In a 5-quart heavy-bottomed Dutch oven or casserole, heat 2 tablespoons of the oil over medium-high heat. Working in batches if necessary, add the fish without crowding the pan and cook, turning once, for about 4 minutes, or until lightly browned. Transfer the fish to a plate and set aside.

In the same casserole, melt the butter with the remaining oil. Add the onion, ginger, jalapeño, garlic, and cinnamon and cook, stirring often, for about 5 minutes, or until the onion is golden and softened. Add the reserved garam masala and stir for 1 minute. Add the rice and stir for another minute.

Add the broth or clam juice mixture and salt and bring to a boil over high heat, scraping up any browned bits on the bottom of the casserole. Reduce the heat to low, cover, and simmer for about 15 minutes, or until the rice is almost tender.

Stir in the tomatoes, cilantro, and fish. Cover, and cook for 2 minutes. Remove the casserole from the heat and let stand, covered, for about 5 minutes, or until all the liquid has been absorbed and the rice is tender. Remove the cinnamon stick and garnish with fresh cilantro. Serve immediately.

1½ teaspoons salt

5 ripe plum tomatoes, cored, seeded & cut into ½-inch pieces

½ cup chopped fresh cilantro, plus additional for garnish

RED & YELLOW PEPPERS STUFFED
WITH WILD RICE & STEAK

SERVES 6

STUFFED BELL PEPPERS DO NOT HAVE TO BE THE
DRIED-OUT, OVERCOOKED FARE OF CAFETERIAS—THEY CAN BE
ABSOLUTELY DELICIOUS AND ELEGANT ENOUGH FOR THE
MOST SOPHISTICATED OCCASION. THESE ARE FILLED WITH A ROBUST,
SPICY MIXTURE OF FLANK STEAK AND A WILD RICE BLEND.

WILD RICE

1½ cups wild rice blend (omitting
seasoning packet)

1 tablespoon chopped fresh
flat-leaf parsley

1 tablespoon chopped fresh
rosemary or 1 teaspoon dried

1 tablespoon chopped fresh thyme
or ¾ teaspoon dried

¼ cup olive oil

1½ pounds flank steak

¼ teaspoon salt

¼ teaspoon freshly ground
black pepper

TOMATO SAUCE

¼ cup dry red wine

1 medium-size onion, chopped

1 garlic clove, minced

1 (28-ounce) can peeled whole
tomatoes in juice

1 tablespoon chopped fresh
flat-leaf parsley

1 tablespoon chopped fresh thyme
or ¾ teaspoon dried

⅛ teaspoon hot pepper flakes

Prepare the rice: Cook the rice blend according to package directions. Stir in the herbs and set aside.

In a large nonreactive skillet, heat 2 tablespoons of the oil over medium-high heat. Season the steak with salt and pepper and cook for about 5 minutes on each side, or until browned. Transfer the meat to a platter and set aside. Pour the fat from the pan.

Prepare the sauce: Add the wine to the skillet, increase the heat to high, and cook, scraping up any browned bits from the bottom of the skillet, for 2 to 3 minutes, or until reduced by about half. Add the onion and cook, stirring frequently, for 5 minutes, or until softened. Add the garlic and cook for 30 seconds, or until aromatic. Stir in the tomatoes with their juice, parsley, thyme, and the ⅛ teaspoon hot pepper flakes. Return the beef to the pan and simmer, partially covered, over medium-low heat for 35 to 45 minutes, or until the meat is tender. Transfer the meat to a clean platter. Pour the sauce into a medium-size nonreactive saucepan. Wipe out the skillet.

Prepare the peppers: Slice off about ½ inch from the stem ends of the peppers. Carefully scoop out the seeds and ribs from the peppers.

Bring a large saucepan of water to a boil over high heat. Set a bowl of cold water near the stove. Working in batches, drop the peppers into boiling water and cook for 5 minutes, until slightly softened.

Using tongs, transfer the peppers to the cold water to stop the cooking. Drain the peppers on paper towels.

Chop the cooked beef into ¼- to ½-inch pieces. Preheat the oven to 375°F.

Heat the remaining 2 tablespoons oil in the same skillet over medium-high heat. Add the onion and celery and cook for 2 to 3 minutes, or until the vegetables begin to soften. Add the garlic and cook, stirring, for 30 seconds, or until aromatic. Add the chopped beef and tomatoes and cook for 2 to 3 minutes, or until the tomatoes soften. Stir in the 1 tablespoon hot pepper flakes or sauce and season with salt and pepper. Stir in the rice mixture.

Spoon the mixture into the peppers, mounding it slightly on top. Arrange the peppers in a baking pan just large enough to hold them snugly. Bake for 20 minutes, or until the filling is heated through. Drape 2 slices of mozzarella over each pepper and sprinkle with Parmesan. Bake for 5 to 10 minutes longer, or until the mozzarella melts.

Meanwhile, reheat the sauce. Serve the peppers and pass the sauce separately.

PEPPERS

3 large red bell peppers

3 large yellow bell peppers

1 small onion, chopped

2 celery stalks, chopped

3 garlic cloves, minced

2 ripe medium-size tomatoes, peeled, cored, seeded & chopped

1 tablespoon hot pepper flakes or hot pepper sauce

Salt & pepper to taste

12 thin slices mozzarella cheese (about 4 ounces)

¼ cup freshly grated Parmesan cheese

THAI FRIED JASMINE RICE
WITH SHRIMP

SERVES 4

YOU MAY USE ANY AROMATIC RICES FOR THIS
QUICK SUPPER DISH, BUT THAI-GROWN JASMINE RICE DOES
BRING AUTHENTICITY. BOTTLED FISH SAUCE
CAN BE FOUND IN THE ETHNIC FOOD SECTION OF YOUR
SUPERMARKET OR IN ASIAN GROCERY STORES.

1⅓ cups jasmine rice

¼ cup chicken broth

2 tablespoons fish sauce, such as
nuoc mam or nam pla

2 tablespoons soy sauce

2 teaspoons sugar

⅛ teaspoon hot pepper flakes

2 tablespoons vegetable oil

8 ounces medium-size shrimp,
peeled & deveined

3 shallots, finely chopped

1 garlic clove, minced

2 large eggs, well beaten

⅓ cup chopped fresh mint
or cilantro

2 green onions, chopped

1 cup bean sprouts

1 large carrot, shredded

¼ cup chopped unsalted
dry-roasted peanuts

Cook the rice following the basic method for steamed rice (p. 11) or according to the package directions. Refrigerate, covered, until thoroughly chilled.

With dampened hands, rub the cold rice between your fingers and palms to separate the grains. Set aside.

In a small bowl, combine the broth, fish sauce, soy sauce, sugar, and hot pepper flakes. Set aside.

In a large nonstick skillet, heat the vegetable oil over medium-high heat. Add the shrimp and cook, stirring often, for about 2 minutes, or until pink and firm. Using a slotted spoon, transfer the shrimp to a plate.

Add the shallots and garlic to the skillet and cook, stirring, for about 1 minute, or until softened. Add the rice and cook for 1 minute. Pour in the broth mixture and cook, stirring, for about 1 minute, or until the rice is evenly coated. Add the eggs and shrimp and cook, stirring, for another 2 to 3 minutes, or until the rice is coated and the eggs are set but not dry. Stir in the chopped mint or cilantro and green onions.

Spoon the fried rice into heated serving bowls and top with the bean sprouts, carrot, and peanuts.

MIDDLE-EASTERN LAMB PILAF

IN THE MIDDLE EAST, HOME COOKS PREPARE DISHES
THAT COMBINE MEAT WITH RICE AND SPICES, AND FREQUENTLY USE
THE CLASSIC SWEET-SPICY COMBINATION OF CINNAMON
AND CUMIN. THE TERM *PILAF* IS DERIVED FROM *PILAV*, THE TURKISH
WORD FOR THIS SIMPLE, ONE-POT FAMILY MEAL.

2 tablespoons olive oil

2 pounds boneless leg of lamb,
trimmed of fat & cut into
1-inch pieces

1¼ teaspoons salt

¼ teaspoon freshly ground
black pepper

2 large onions, halved lengthwise
& sliced crosswise
¼ inch thick

2 medium-size carrots, cut into
½-inch-thick rounds

2 garlic cloves, minced

½ teaspoon cinnamon

½ teaspoon ground cumin

2 cups long-grain white rice

½ cup packed dried apricots

3 tablespoons chopped fresh
flat-leaf parsley

In a 5-quart nonreactive Dutch oven or casserole, heat the oil over medium-high heat. Working in batches, add the lamb and cook, stirring frequently, for 5 to 6 minutes, or until browned on all sides. Transfer to a plate and season with ½ teaspoon of the salt and the pepper.

Add the onions, carrots, and garlic to the pot. Reduce the heat to medium and cook, stirring often, for about 5 minutes, or until the onions are softened. Return the meat and any accumulated juices to the pot. Stir in the cinnamon and cumin, add 4 cups water, and bring to a boil. Reduce the heat to low, cover, and simmer for about 1 hour, or until the meat is just tender.

Strain the stew in a colander set over a large bowl. Skim the fat from the cooking liquid. You should have 4 cups of liquid; add water if necessary.

Return the meat, vegetables, and cooking liquid to the pot and stir in the rice, apricots, and the remaining ¾ teaspoon salt. Bring to a boil over high heat. Reduce the heat to low, cover, and simmer for about 20 minutes, or until the rice is tender and all the liquid has been absorbed. Stir in the parsley. Let stand, covered, for 5 minutes. Transfer the pilaf to a heated serving bowl, fluff the rice with a large spoon, and serve.

GINGER-COCONUT RICE
WITH CILANTRO

S E R V E S 6

THROUGHOUT INDONESIA AND SOUTHEAST ASIA, RICE IS

COMMONLY COOKED WITH COCONUT MILK FOR ITS PLEASING SWEETNESS,

EVEN WHEN THE MAIN DISH IS DEFINITELY SAVORY. THIS VERSION

HAS SPICY UNDERTONES TO OFFSET THE SWEETNESS AND IS DELICIOUS WITH

BROILED OR GRILLED MEATS OR CHICKEN OR WITH ROASTED PORK.

To toast coconut, spread it on a baking sheet and toast in a preheated 350°F oven, shaking the pan once or twice for even toasting, for 2 to 3 minutes, or until aromatic and lightly browned. Transfer to a plate to cool.

In a large nonreactive skillet, heat the oils over medium-high heat. Add the onion and bell pepper and cook for 2 to 3 minutes, or until they begin to soften. Add the garlic and ginger and cook for 1 minute, or until aromatic. Stir in the rice and cook, stirring, for 3 to 4 minutes, or until the rice is coated with oil and just begins to brown.

Stir in the broth, 1 cup water, and the coconut milk. Reduce the heat, cover, and simmer for 15 to 20 minutes, or until all the liquid has been absorbed. Remove the pan from the heat and let stand, covered, for 10 minutes, or until the rice is tender. Stir in the green onions, cilantro, coconut flakes, and lemon juice, and serve immediately.

2 tablespoons unsweetened coconut flakes

2 tablespoons peanut oil

1 tablespoon hot chile oil

1 small onion, chopped

1 medium-size red bell pepper, cored, seeded & diced

2 garlic cloves, minced

1 tablespoon minced peeled fresh ginger

1½ cups medium-grain white rice

1½ cups chicken broth

½ cup canned coconut milk

3 green onions, chopped

¼ cup chopped fresh cilantro

¼ cup fresh lemon juice

LEMON-OREGANO RICE

SERVES 4 TO 6

THIS SIMPLE HERBED RICE IS PERFECT WITH GRILLED LAMB OR
PORK, BUT IT CAN BE VARIED DEPENDING ON WHAT YOU ARE SERVING:
WITH CHICKEN, USE CHICKEN BROTH; WITH FISH, FISH
BROTH; WITH A MEATLESS MEAL, VEGETABLE BROTH. AND TRY
DIFFERENT HERBS, SUCH AS DILL OR TARRAGON.

Grate the zest from the lemon into a 2-cup liquid measuring cup. Squeeze the lemon juice and strain it through a fine-mesh sieve into the cup. Add the broth and enough water to make 2 cups of liquid. Stir in the salt and pepper. If using dried oregano, add it now.

In a medium-size saucepan, melt the butter over medium heat. Add the green onions and cook, stirring often, for about 2 minutes, or until wilted. Add the rice and stir for about 1 minute, or until the grains turn chalky-white. Stir in the broth mixture and bring to a boil over high heat. Cover tightly, reduce the heat to low, and simmer for about 20 minutes, or until the rice is tender and all the liquid has been absorbed.

Stir in the fresh oregano if using. Remove the saucepan from the heat and let the rice stand, covered, for 5 minutes. Transfer the rice to a heated serving bowl and fluff with a fork. Garnish with long, thin strips of lemon zest.

1 lemon

1 cup beef broth

½ teaspoon salt

¼ teaspoon freshly ground black pepper

1 tablespoon minced fresh oregano or 1 teaspoon dried

2 tablespoons unsalted butter

2 green onions, chopped

1 cup long-grain white rice

Lemon zest, for garnish

GOLDEN-CRUSTED PERSIAN RICE

S E R V E S   6

THE CRISP, GOLDEN RICE CRUST THAT FORMS ON THE BOTTOM
OF THE COOKING POT IS A DELICACY IN IRAN, AND THE METHOD USED HERE
ENSURES THAT THE RICE WILL BROWN, NOT BURN. COMMONLY
SERVED WITH SHISH KEBABS AND STEWS, THIS DISH CAN BE DRESSED UP
WITH CHICKEN OR SHRIMP FOR A MORE SUBSTANTIAL MEAL.

Bring a large pot of generously salted water to a boil over high heat. Add the rice and boil for 7 to 8 minutes, or until barely tender. Drain, rinse under cold running water, and drain again.

In a heavy-bottomed medium-size saucepan, melt the butter with the oil over medium heat. Remove half of the fat and set aside, then remove the pan from the heat.

Add 2 tablespoons water and rice to the saucepan. Pour the reserved fat over the rice. Lay a double thickness of moistened cheesecloth on the rice, cover tightly, and cook for 15 minutes over low heat. Increase the heat to medium-low and cook for 5 minutes longer, or until the rice is tender and a golden crust has formed on the bottom of the pan. Remove from the heat and let stand for 5 minutes.

Using a large spoon, scrape up the rice crust from the bottom of the pan, mixing it with the rest of the rice. Transfer the rice to a heated bowl or platter and serve.

2 cups basmati rice

4 tablespoons (½ stick) unsalted butter

2 tablespoons vegetable oil

BAKED LOUISIANA RED RICE

SERVES 4 TO 6

RICE SIMMERED WITH TOMATOES AND SEASONINGS IS A
FAVORITE SIDE DISH IN LOUISIANA BAYOU COUNTRY. LONG-GRAIN
RICE IS THE ONE MOST OFTEN USED IN LOUISIANA,
ALTHOUGH AROMATIC BASMATI-STYLE RICES, ALSO GROWN THERE,
ARE POPULAR FOR THIS DISH.

1 (15-ounce) can whole tomatoes in juice, drained & seeded

2 tablespoons olive oil

1 small onion, chopped

½ cup chopped green bell pepper

1 cup long-grain white rice

1 garlic clove, minced

1½ cups chicken broth

½ teaspoon dried basil

½ teaspoon dried thyme

½ teaspoon salt

⅛ teaspoon cayenne, or to taste

Preheat the oven to 350°F. Lightly oil a 1½-quart round baking dish.

In a blender, process the tomatoes to a purée.

In a medium-size nonreactive saucepan, heat the oil over medium heat. Add the onion and bell pepper and cook, stirring often, for about 5 minutes, or until the onion is softened. Add the rice and garlic and cook, stirring, for about 2 minutes, or until the rice grains turn chalky-white. Stir in the broth, tomato purée, basil, thyme, salt, and cayenne. Bring to a simmer. Transfer to the prepared baking dish and cover tightly.

Bake for 20 to 25 minutes, or until the rice is tender and all the liquid has been absorbed. Remove from the oven and let stand for 5 minutes. Fluff with a fork and serve immediately.

VARIATIONS

• *Baked Louisiana Red Rice with Shrimp:* Stir 8 ounces shelled deveined hot cooked shrimp into the rice just before serving.

• *Baked Louisiana Red Rice with Ham:* Stir 8 ounces diced cooked ham into the rice before serving.

SPICY MALAYSIAN RICE

S E R V E S 6

IN MALAYSIA, THIS SPICY RICE, *NASI GORENG,*
IS OFTEN SERVED WITH STIR-FRIED CHICKEN OR BEEF. HERE,
IT IS MIXED WITH RED BELL PEPPER AND OTHER
VEGETABLES TO CREATE A DELICIOUS SIDE DISH FOR SIMPLE
GRILLED OR ROASTED MEAT, POULTRY, OR FISH.

Prepare the rice following the basic method for boiled rice (p. 13) or steamed rice (p. 11) or according to the package directions. Transfer to a large bowl to cool to room temperature. Cover with plastic wrap and refrigerate for at least 4 hours, or until thoroughly chilled.

In a food processor fitted with the metal blade or in a blender, combine the bell pepper, onion, jalapeño, garlic, and anchovy paste or anchovy fillets and process until smooth.

Heat a wok or skillet over medium-high heat. Add 2 tablespoons of the oil to the pan and swirl to coat. Add the bell pepper purée and cook, stirring often, for 4 to 5 minutes, or until the mixture thickens to a paste. Add the remaining 2 tablespoons oil and swirl the pan to coat. Add the rice and stir-fry for 1 minute. Add the soy sauce and stir-fry for 1 to 2 minutes longer, or until the rice is heated through.

Arrange the shredded lettuce on a serving platter. Spoon the rice mixture over the lettuce and top with the tomato wedges and sliced cucumber and green onions. Serve immediately.

1¼ cups long-grain white rice

1 medium-size red bell pepper, cored, seeded & chopped

1 medium-size onion, chopped

1 jalapeño or hot chile pepper, seeded & chopped

2 garlic cloves, minced

1 teaspoon anchovy paste or diced canned anchovy fillets

¼ cup vegetable oil

2 tablespoons soy sauce

3 cups shredded romaine lettuce

1 tomato, cut into 6 wedges

1 medium-size cucumber, peeled & thinly sliced crosswise

2 green onions, thinly sliced

RICE WITH ROASTED RED PEPPERS, BLACK OLIVES & FETA

SERVES 6

THE WONDERFUL, VIVID COLORS—RED BELL
PEPPER, GREEN ONION AND PARSLEY, BLACK CALAMATA
OLIVES—SIGNAL THE LIVELY FLAVORS OF
THIS SIDE DISH. OLIVES AND FETA MAY PRECLUDE
THE NEED FOR SALT.

1 large red bell pepper

1½ cups long-grain white rice

1 tablespoon olive oil

2 to 3 green onions, chopped

1 garlic clove, minced

¼ cup chopped fresh
flat-leaf parsley

2 tablespoons fresh lemon juice

3 tablespoons chopped sun-dried
tomatoes packed in oil

3 tablespoons chopped pitted
Calamata or other
brine-cured olives

¼ teaspoon freshly ground
black pepper

4 ounces feta cheese, cut into
6 slices

Sprigs of fresh flat-leaf parsley,
for garnish (optional)

Preheat the broiler with the pan 6 inches from the heat source. Place the bell pepper on the broiler pan and broil, turning frequently, for about 10 to 15 minutes, or until blackened on all sides. Transfer to a paper bag, close the bag, and let cool. Halve the pepper, core, seed, peel, and chop.

Cook the long-grain rice following the basic method for steamed rice (p. 11) or according to the package directions.

Meanwhile, in a small skillet, heat the oil over medium heat. Add the green onions and cook, stirring frequently, for 3 to 4 minutes, or until softened. Add the garlic and cook for 1 minute, or until aromatic. Add the parsley, lemon juice, sun-dried tomatoes, olives, pepper, and bell pepper and cook, stirring, for 1 to 2 minutes, until the ingredients are just heated through.

Toss the hot rice with the bell pepper mixture. Transfer the rice to heated bowls and serve immediately, garnished with the feta and fresh parsley, if desired.

WILD RICE, CHESTNUT
& APPLE DRESSING

MAKES ABOUT 8 CUPS, 8 TO 12 SERVINGS

WHILE A STUFFING MAY BE USED TO FILL THE
CAVITY OF A BIRD, A DRESSING IS MEANT TO BE SERVED ON
THE SIDE. THIS PUNGENT WILD RICE DRESSING
CAN SERVE AS EITHER; THE RECIPE MAKES MORE THAN ENOUGH
TO STUFF A TWELVE- TO SIXTEEN-POUND TURKEY.

1 pound fresh chestnuts,
    or vacuum-packed
    peeled chestnuts

3 tablespoons unsalted butter

1 large onion, chopped

1 large celery stalk, cut into
    ½-inch pieces

1 Granny Smith or other tart
    cooking apple, peeled, cored
    & cut into ½-inch pieces

2¾ cups (about 1 pound)
    wild rice, rinsed

4 cups chicken broth

1 cup apple cider

1 teaspoon dried thyme

½ teaspoon salt

¼ teaspoon freshly
    ground black pepper

If using fresh chestnuts, preheat the oven to 400°F.

Using a sharp paring knife, cut an "X" in the flat side of each chestnut, piercing the thick skin. Spread the chestnuts on a baking sheet and bake, shaking the pan occasionally, for about 30 minutes, or until the skins have cracked open and the nutmeat is tender and golden brown. While the chestnuts are still warm, peel off the thick outer skins and the thin inner peels. Coarsely chop the chestnuts and set aside.

In a large nonreactive saucepan, melt the butter over medium heat. Add the onion, celery, and apple and cook, stirring often, for about 8 minutes, or until the onion is softened.

Stir in the wild rice, broth, apple cider, thyme, salt, and pepper. Bring to a boil over high heat, reduce the heat to low, cover, and cook for about 1 hour, or until the wild rice is tender. The cooking time depends on the age of the rice; begin checking for doneness after 45 minutes. The rice is done when the outer hulls crack, exposing the white interiors. During the last 5 minutes of cooking, stir in the chopped chestnuts. Drain the rice if necessary. Serve hot, or let cool completely and use to stuff a turkey.

NEW ORLEANS RICE FRITTERS

SERVES 6 TO 8

IN NEW ORLEANS, THERE IS GREAT FONDNESS FOR THESE
RICE FRITTERS, CALLED *CALAS*. THESE USE COOKED LONG-GRAIN RICE,
AND RICE FLOUR TO KEEP THE TEXTURE LIGHT. EAT THEM
WARM, WITH A SPRINKLING OF CONFECTIONERS' SUGAR, YOUR FAVORITE
JELLY, OR DRIZZLED WITH HONEY.

In a medium-size saucepan, bring 3 cups water to a boil over medium heat. Add the rice and cook until the rice is very soft and the water is almost absorbed, about 25 minutes. Drain and let cool.

In a small bowl, dissolve ¼ teaspoon of the granulated sugar in the warm water. Sprinkle the yeast over the water and let stand for 5 to 10 minutes, or until foamy. Stir to dissolve the yeast.

In a medium-size bowl, mash the rice with the back of a spoon. Stir in the yeast mixture, then beat in the eggs, the remaining ⅓ cup sugar, orange zest, cinnamon, nutmeg, and salt. Add the rice flour and stir to a smooth, thick batter. Cover and let rise in a warm, draft-free place for 1¼ hours, or until almost doubled in volume.

Preheat the oven to 200°F. Heat 2 inches of oil in a deep-fat fryer or large deep skillet to 370°F, or until a cube of bread browns within one minute.

Stir the batter to deflate it. Slide heaping tablespoons of batter, without crowding, into the hot oil and fry, turning once, for about 4 minutes, or until golden brown. Adjust the oil temperature so the fritters cook in 4 minutes or less. Transfer the fritters to a paper-towel-lined baking sheet and blot with paper towels. Keep warm in the oven and continue, stirring the batter well between batches.

Sift confectioners' sugar over the warm fritters.

½ cup long-grain white rice

⅓ cup plus ¼ teaspoon granulated sugar

¼ cup warm (105° to 115°F) water

1 (¼-ounce) package active dry yeast

3 large eggs

Grated zest of 1 large orange

¼ teaspoon cinnamon

½ teaspoon grated nutmeg

½ teaspoon salt

1½ cups rice flour or brown rice flour

Vegetable oil, for deep-frying

Confectioners' sugar, for dusting

WILD RICE & MUSHROOM PANCAKES

LIKE THEIR COUSIN THE POTATO PANCAKE,
THESE SKILLET CAKES CAN BE SATISFYING FOR BRUNCH
OR SUPPER. THE NUTTY, EARTHY FLAVOR OF
WILD RICE PAIRS WELL WITH SOUR CREAM. SERVE THIS
WITH ROAST PORK OR VENISON.

1 cup wild rice, rinsed

3 cups chicken broth

2 tablespoons unsalted butter,
plus more for the griddle

10 ounces mushrooms, very
finely chopped

1 medium-size onion, finely
chopped

½ cup unbleached
all-purpose flour

⅓ cup heavy cream

2 large eggs

1 tablespoon chopped fresh sage
or 1 teaspoon dried

½ teaspoon salt

¼ teaspoon freshly ground
black pepper

Sour cream, for garnish (optional)

Cook the wild rice in the broth, following the basic method for wild rice (p. 15) or according to the package directions. Let cool.

In a medium-size skillet, melt the butter over medium heat. Add the mushrooms and onion and cook, stirring often, for 8 to 10 minutes, or until the liquid has evaporated and the mixture is quite dry. Remove the pan from the heat and set aside.

Preheat the oven to 200°F.

In a large bowl, whisk together the flour, cream, eggs, sage, salt, and pepper until smooth. Add the wild rice and the mushroom mixture and stir well.

Preheat a lightly buttered griddle or large skillet over medium heat. When hot, ladle about ¼ cup batter for each pancake onto the griddle, spreading the batter with a spatula into 3-inch-wide pancakes. Cook the pancakes for 2 to 3 minutes, or until the undersides are browned. Flip the pancakes and cook for about 2 minutes longer, or until browned. Transfer the cooked pancakes to a baking sheet and keep warm in the preheated oven while you cook the remaining pancakes. Arrange the hot pancakes on a heated platter and serve with sour cream if desired.

WILD RICE RYE BREAD

THE EARTHY FLAVORS OF WILD RICE AND
RYE FLOUR BLEND HARMONIOUSLY IN THIS DELICIOUS
SANDWICH OR TOASTING LOAF, ONE TASTE
NEVER OVERPOWERING THE OTHER. THE RICE ALSO
GIVES TEXTURE TO THIS HOMEY BREAD.

½ cup wild rice, rinsed

1 teaspoon sugar

1¼ cups warm
(105° to 115°F) water

1 (¼ ounce) package active
dry yeast

1 cup rye flour

About 2½ cups unbleached
all-purpose flour

1 teaspoon salt

1 tablespoon vegetable oil

1 tablespoon honey

Cook the rice following the basic method for wild rice (p. 15) or according to the package directions. Let cool.

In a small bowl, dissolve the sugar in the warm water. Sprinkle the yeast over the water and let stand for 5 to 10 minutes, or until foamy. Stir to dissolve the yeast.

In a large bowl, combine the rye flour, 1½ cups all-purpose flour, the salt, oil, and honey. Add the yeast mixture and stir, adding more all-purpose flour as necessary to make a soft dough that pulls away from the sides of the bowl.

Turn the dough out onto a work surface lightly floured with all-purpose flour and knead for about 10 minutes, adding more flour as needed to form a dough that is smooth and elastic yet slightly sticky.

Shape the dough into a ball, place in a lightly buttered bowl, and turn to coat. Cover the bowl with plastic wrap and let rise in a warm, draft-free place for about 1½ hours, or until it has almost doubled in volume.

Butter a 9- by 5-inch loaf pan. Punch the dough down. Turn the dough out onto a work surface lightly floured with all-purpose flour and knead 4 or 5 times. Flatten the dough into a rectangle, about 12- by 9-inches, and spread the wild rice over the dough. Fold the dough over in

half and knead for 2 to 3 minutes, or until the rice is evenly distributed throughout the dough. Shape the dough into a loaf and place in the prepared loaf pan. Cover with plastic wrap and let rise in a warm, draft-free place for about 45 minutes, or until it has almost doubled in volume.

Preheat the oven to 350°F.

With a razor blade or very sharp knife, score the top of the loaf down the center. Bake for 30 to 35 minutes, or until the loaf is lightly browned and sounds hollow when tapped on the bottom. Transfer the pan to a wire rack to cool for about 5 minutes. Turn the loaf out onto the rack and let cool completely before slicing.

BROWN RICE & ROSEMARY
DINNER ROLLS

MAKES 15 ROLLS

PERFUMED WITH FRESH ROSEMARY, THESE RICH,
FILLING ROLLS HAVE AN EXTRA-CHEWY TEXTURE, IDEAL FOR
SOUP AND CASSEROLE SUPPERS. FOR HEARTY
SANDWICHES, SHAPE THE DOUGH INTO LARGER ROLLS, AND
INCREASE THE BAKING TIME A FEW MINUTES.

⅓ cup long- or medium-grain
　　brown rice

1 cup milk

4 tablespoons (½ stick) unsalted
　　butter, cut into pieces,
　　plus 2 tablespoons, melted

2 tablespoons honey

1½ teaspoons salt

1 (¼-ounce) package active
　　dry yeast

3 tablespoons warm
　　(105° to 115°F) water

1 large egg

1 tablespoon chopped
　　fresh rosemary or
　　1½ teaspoons dried

1 cup whole-wheat flour

½ cup brown rice flour

About 2 cups all-purpose flour

Cook the rice following the basic method for boiled brown rice (p. 13) or according to the package directions. Let cool.

In a small saucepan, bring the milk just to a simmer. Stir in the 4 tablespoons butter, honey, and salt and immediately remove from the heat. Let the mixture stand until lukewarm.

In a small bowl, sprinkle the yeast over the warm water and let stand for about 10 minutes, or until foamy. Stir to dissolve the yeast.

In a large bowl, beat the egg. Gradually beat in the lukewarm milk mixture. Stir in the yeast mixture, rice, and rosemary. Stir in the whole-wheat and rice flours, then gradually beat in enough of the all-purpose flour to make a soft dough that pulls away from the sides of the bowl.

Turn the dough out onto a work surface lightly floured with all-purpose flour and knead for about 10 minutes, adding only as much flour as necessary to keep the dough from sticking. The dough should become supple and elastic but remain slightly sticky.

Shape the dough into a ball, place in a lightly buttered bowl, and turn to coat. Cover the bowl with plastic wrap and let rise in a warm, draft-free place for about 1½ hours, or until almost doubled in volume.

Lightly butter a large baking sheet. Punch down the dough and turn out onto a lightly floured

work surface. Shape the dough into fifteen 2-inch balls and arrange them 2 inches apart on the prepared baking sheet. Cover with plastic wrap and let stand in a warm, draft-free place for about 45 minutes, or until almost doubled in volume.

Preheat the oven to 400°F.

Brush the tops of the rolls with the 2 tablespoons melted butter. Bake for about 20 minutes, or until the rolls are golden brown and sound hollow when tapped on the bottom. Transfer to wire racks to cool for at least 10 minutes before serving.

RICE & CURRANT PANCAKES WITH RASPBERRY-MAPLE SYRUP

ORDINARY PANCAKES WILL PALE IN
COMPARISON TO THESE HEARTY RICE GRIDDLE CAKES. THEIR
CHARACTER DEPENDS ON THE TYPE OF RICE YOU
USE, SO FEEL FREE TO EXPERIMENT WITH BASMATI, BROWN,
OR JASMINE RICE—ALL ARE TASTY.

RASPBERRY-MAPLE SYRUP

1 ½ cups fresh or frozen
    unsweetened raspberries,
    thawed

¾ cup pure maple syrup

3 tablespoons unsalted butter,
    cut into pieces

¼ cup long-grain white rice

1 ¼ cups unbleached
    all-purpose flour

2 tablespoons sugar

1 teaspoon baking powder

1 teaspoon baking soda

¼ teaspoon salt

1 cup plain low-fat yogurt

¾ cup milk

2 large eggs

3 tablespoons unsalted
    butter, melted

½ cup dried currants

½ cup fresh raspberries,
    for garnish

Prepare the syrup: In a blender or a food processor fitted with the metal blade, pureé the raspberries and syrup. Transfer to a medium-size nonreactive saucepan. Bring to a simmer over medium heat and simmer for 2 minutes. Strain through a sieve to remove the seeds and return the purée to the pan. Stir in the butter over low heat until melted. Set aside. Preheat the oven to 200°F.

Cook the rice in water following the basic method for boiled rice (p. 13), or according to the package directions. Let cool.

Sift together the flour, sugar, baking powder, baking soda, and salt into a large bowl.

In a medium-size bowl, whisk together the yogurt, milk, eggs, and butter. Stir into the flour mixture just until barely smooth; a few small lumps should remain. Fold in the rice and currants.

Lightly grease a large griddle or skillet and heat over medium heat until hot. Pour ¼ cup batter onto the hot griddle for each pancake. Cook for about 2 minutes, or until tiny holes form on the tops of the pancakes and the edges are set. Flip the pancakes and cook until the undersides are golden brown. Transfer to a heatproof plate and keep warm in the oven while you cook the remaining pancakes.

Serve hot with the syrup and raspberries spooned on top.

FRENCH RICE PUDDING WITH RASPBERRY SAUCE

SERVES 8 TO 10

IN ITS ORIGINAL FORM, THIS DESSERT IS A
COMPLICATED AFFAIR NAMED *RIZ À L'IMPÉRATRICE*, OR "THE
EMPRESS'S RICE." THIS IS A STREAMLINED VERSION.
LONG-GRAIN WHITE RICE WORKS BEST, AS THE GRAINS REMAIN
FIRM AND SEPARATE DURING COOKING.

RICE PUDDING

½ cup dried cherries or
    dried currants

¼ cup dark rum

1 quart milk

¾ cup sugar

½ cup long-grain white rice

¼ teaspoon salt

1 envelope (a scant tablespoon)
    unflavored gelatin

6 large egg yolks

1 teaspoon vanilla extract

1 cup heavy cream, chilled

RASPBERRY SAUCE

2 pints fresh raspberries or
    1 (12-ounce) bag frozen
    unsweetened raspberries,
    thawed & drained

¼ cup sugar

2 tablespoons fresh lemon juice

2 tablespoons raspberry-flavored
    liqueur, such as Chambord, or
    raspberry-flavored syrup

Prepare the pudding: In a small bowl, combine the cherries or currants and rum. Let stand for about 1 hour, or until the fruit is plump.

In a medium-size saucepan, combine the milk, sugar, rice, and salt and bring to a simmer, stirring constantly, over medium heat. Reduce the heat to low and gently simmer, stirring often to avoid sticking, for 20 to 25 minutes, or until the rice is tender.

In a small bowl, sprinkle the gelatin over ¼ cup water and let stand 5 to 10 minutes, or until the gelatin is softened.

Meanwhile, in a medium-size bowl, whisk the yolks until blended. Gradually whisk in the hot rice mixture. Return the mixture to the pan and cook, stirring constantly, over low heat for about 2 minutes, or until very thick; do not allow to simmer. An instant-read thermometer should register 170°F. Remove the pan from the heat. Stir the gelatin mixture into the rice mixture; stir to dissolve the gelatin.

Scrape the rice mixture into a bowl and place in a larger bowl of ice water. Stir in the cherries or currants with the soaking liquid and the vanilla. Let stand, stirring occasionally, for 10 to 15 minutes, or until cooled but not set.

In a chilled medium-size bowl, beat the heavy cream until stiff. Fold into the rice mixture. Pour

into a lightly oiled 6- to 7-cup fluted tube pan. Cover the surface directly with plastic wrap and refrigerate until set, at least 6 hours or overnight.

Prepare the sauce: In a food processor fitted with the metal blade or in a blender, combine all the ingredients and process to a purée. Strain through a fine-mesh sieve into a small bowl to remove the seeds. Cover and refrigerate until ready to serve.

To serve, run a small sharp knife around the inside of the rice mold. Hold the pan in a large bowl of hot water for 5 seconds to release the pudding. Dry the outside of the pan and invert the pudding onto a chilled platter. Slice into wedges and serve with the raspberry sauce.

FRUIT-STUDDED RICE PUDDING

SERVES 6 TO 8

RAISINS TEND TO BE THE FRUIT OF CHOICE
FOR THIS HOMESPUN DESSERT BUT OTHER DRIED FRUITS SUCH
AS CHERRIES, BLUEBERRIES, AND CRANBERRIES ADD THEIR
OWN SWEET FLAIR. THE PUDDING CAN BE BAKED IN SIX 8-OUNCE
CUSTARD CUPS, IN THE WATER BATH FOR 45 MINUTES.

Cook the rice in water following the basic method for boiled rice (p. 13), or according to the package directions.

Preheat the oven to 325°F. Lightly butter an 11- by 7-inch baking dish.

In a medium-size saucepan, combine the milk, half-and-half, and sugar. Heat over medium heat, stirring frequently to dissolve the sugar, for about 5 minutes, or until small bubbles appear around the edges of the pan. Remove from the heat.

In a large bowl, whisk together the eggs and vanilla and almond extracts. Slowly whisk the hot milk mixture into the eggs. Stir in the rice and dried fruit. Pour into the baking dish and sprinkle with the cinnamon if desired.

Set the baking dish in a larger pan and put the pan in the oven. Add enough hot water to the larger pan to come halfway up the sides of the baking dish. Bake for 50 to 60 minutes, or until a knife inserted in the center of the pudding comes out clean. Let cool. Serve warm or refrigerate and serve chilled, garnished with blueberries and mint.

½ cup long-grain white rice

2 cups milk

1 cup half-and-half

½ cup sugar

6 large eggs

½ teaspoon vanilla extract

½ teaspoon almond extract

½ cup dried blueberries, cherries, cranberries, or raisins

¼ teaspoon cinnamon (optional)

Fresh blueberries and mint leaves, for garnish (optional)

COCONUT-GINGER TORTE

THIS RICH, MOIST, PUDDING-LIKE CAKE IS INSPIRED
BY THE DESSERTS OF SOUTHEAST ASIA, AND GETS ITS SOFT, CREAMY
TEXTURE FROM THE STICKY RICE. THE CAKE WOULD
TASTE GOOD AFTER ANY MEAL BUT IS PARTICULARLY DELICIOUS
AFTER SPICY THAI OR VIETNAMESE FOOD.

¾ cup sticky or glutinous rice

¼ teaspoon salt

¼ cup boiling water

1 cup unblanched sliced
    almonds, lightly toasted

1 tablespoon unsalted butter,
    at room temperature

2 (14-ounce) cans coconut milk

1 cup sugar

5 large eggs

Grated zest of 1 lime

½ teaspoon vanilla extract

¾ cup chopped crystallized ginger

Place the rice in a fine-mesh sieve and rinse under cold running water until the water runs almost clear. Transfer to a medium-size bowl and add cold water to cover by 2 inches. Let stand for at least 6 hours or overnight.

Place a steamer insert in a medium-size saucepan and add enough water to almost reach the bottom of the insert. Line the insert with a double thickness of moistened cheesecloth. Drain the rice and place in the steamer. Bring the water in the saucepan to a boil over high heat, cover the pan, and cook for 10 minutes.

Dissolve the salt in ¼ cup boiling water. Sprinkle the boiling water over the rice, reduce the heat to medium-high, cover, and cook for about 10 minutes longer, or until the rice is tender. Transfer the rice to a shallow bowl and let cool completely.

In a food processor fitted with the metal blade, process the almonds until finely ground.

Grease a 10-inch springform pan with the butter and sprinkle with ¼ cup of the ground almonds, tilting the pan to coat the bottom and halfway up the sides. Wrap the outside bottom and side of the pan tightly with a double layer of foil.

In a medium-size nonreactive heavy-bottomed saucepan, combine the rice, coconut milk, and

sugar. Bring to a simmer over medium-high heat, stirring often to avoid sticking. Reduce the heat to low and simmer, stirring frequently, for about 10 minutes, or until the rice is soft. Transfer the rice mixture to the bowl of an electric mixer and let cool for about 45 minutes, or until tepid.

Preheat the oven to 325°F. With the mixer set at medium-high speed, beat in the eggs, 1 at a time. Beat in the zest and vanilla. Stir in the remaining almonds and the ginger. Scrape the batter into the prepared pan.

Set the springform pan in a larger baking pan and add enough hot water to come 1 inch up the side of the springform pan. Bake for about 1 hour, or until the top is golden brown and a knife inserted 2 inches from the side comes out clean. Transfer the pan to a wire rack to cool completely. Serve at room temperature or chilled.

ITALIAN RICE TART

SERVES 8

THIS IS THE SORT OF RUSTIC TART YOU WILL FIND
AT AN OUT-OF-THE-WAY TRATTORIA IN AN ITALIAN COUNTRY VILLAGE.
IT'S MADE WITH A MEDIUM-GRAIN ITALIAN RICE SUCH AS
ARBORIO, WHICH GUARANTEES ITS CREAMY TEXTURE. SERVE AT ROOM
TEMPERATURE TO FULLY APPRECIATE THE FLAVORS.

Prepare the filling: In a small bowl, combine the raisins and liqueur or orange juice and let stand for 1 hour, or until the raisins are plump.

In a medium-size nonreactive saucepan, combine the milk, rice, sugar, and butter and bring to a simmer over medium heat, stirring almost constantly. Reduce the heat to low and gently simmer for about 25 minutes, or until the rice is very tender. Remove from the heat and let cool completely.

In a medium-size bowl, whisk together the eggs, raisins with their soaking liquid, and the vanilla. Whisk in the cooled rice mixture.

Meanwhile, prepare the crust: In a food processor fitted with the metal blade, combine the flour, sugar, and salt and pulse to combine. Add the butter and pulse until the mixture resembles coarse meal. With the machine running, add the egg yolk mixture through the feed tube and process just until the dough holds together when pinched between the thumb and forefinger. If the dough seems too dry, sprinkle with 1 to 2 teaspoons cold water and pulse briefly. Do not overprocess.

(Alternatively, mix together the flour, sugar, and salt in a bowl. Using a pastry blender, two forks, or your fingertips, cut in the butter until the mixture resembles coarse meal. Stir in the egg yolk mixture, mixing only until the dough holds

CUSTARD FILLING

¼ cup seedless golden raisins

2 tablespoons orange-flavored liqueur, such as Grand Marnier, or fresh orange juice

2 cups milk

¼ cup Arborio or other medium-grain Italian rice

¼ cup sugar

2 tablespoons unsalted butter

2 large eggs

¼ teaspoon vanilla extract

SWEET TART CRUST

1 cup all-purpose flour

3 tablespoons sugar

⅛ teaspoon salt

6 tablespoons unsalted butter, chilled & cut into pieces

1 large egg yolk beaten with 1 tablespoon water

APRICOT GLAZE

½ cup apricot preserves

1 tablespoon orange-flavored liqueur, such as Grand Marnier, or fresh orange juice

together when pinched between the thumb and forefinger. If the dough seems too dry, sprinkle with 1 to 2 teaspoons cold water and mix briefly.)

Transfer the dough to a 9-inch fluted tart pan with a removable bottom. Press the dough firmly and evenly over the bottom and up the side of the pan. Cover the shell with plastic wrap and freeze for about 30 minutes.

Preheat the oven to 350°F. Pour the custard into the prepared tart shell, smoothing the top, and place on a baking sheet. Bake for 35 to 40 minutes, or until the filling is puffed and very lightly browned. Transfer the tart to a wire rack to cool for 5 minutes.

Meanwhile, prepare the glaze: In a small non-reactive saucepan, melt the preserves with the liqueur or orange juice over medium-low heat, stirring often. Reduce the heat to low and simmer gently, stirring often, for about 2 minutes, or until the last drops falling from a spoon are very thick and sticky. Push the glaze with the back of a spoon through a sieve into a small bowl. Immediately brush the glaze over the warm tart. Let cool. Serve at room temperature.

INDEX

CONVERSION TABLE

WEIGHTS

ounces & pounds	metric equivalents
¼ ounce	7 grams
⅓ ounce	10 g
½ ounce	14 g
1 ounce	28 g
1½ ounces	42 g
1¾ ounces	50 g
2 ounces	57 g
3 ounces	85 g
3½ ounces	100 g
4 ounces (¼ pound)	114 g
6 ounces	170 g
8 ounces (½ pound)	227 g
9 ounces	250 g
16 ounces (1 pound)	464 g

TEMPERATURES

°F (Fahrenheit)	°C (Celsius or Centigrade)
32 (water freezes)	0
200	93.3
212 (water boils)	100
250	120
275	135
300 (slow oven)	150
325	160
350 (moderate oven)	175
375	190
400 (hot oven)	205
425	220
450 (very hot oven)	233
475	245
500 (extremely hot oven)	260

LIQUID MEASURES

spoons & cups	metric equivalents
¼ teaspoon	1.23 mm
½ teaspoon	2.5 mm
¾ teaspoon	3.7 mm
1 teaspoon	5 mm
1 dessertspoon	10 mm
1 tablespoon (3 teaspoons)	15 mm
2 tablespoons (1 ounce)	30 mm
¼ cup	60 mm
⅓ cup	80 mm
½ cup	120 mm
⅔ cup	160 mm
¾ cup	180 mm
1 cup (8 ounces)	240 mm
2 cups (1 pint)	480 mm
3 cups	710 mm
4 cups (1 quart)	1 liter
4 quarts (1 gallon)	3¾ liters

LENGTH

U.S. measurements	metric equivalents
⅛ inch	3 mm
¼ inch	6 mm
⅜ inch	1 cm
½ inch	1.2 cm
¾ inch	2 cm
1 inch	2.5 cm
1¼ inches	3.1 cm
1½ inches	3.7 cm
2 inches	5 cm
3 inches	7.5 cm
4 inches	10 cm
5 inches	12.5 cm

APPROXIMATE EQUIVALENTS

1 kilo is slightly more than 2 pounds
1 liter is slightly more than 1 quart
1 meter is slightly over 3 feet
1 centimeter is approximately ⅜ inch